The Prayer of Freedom™
Group Study Workbook

A step-by-step guide to freedom
from emotional trauma,
chronic pain and addictions

by
Beatty Carmichael
Published by Maran Ministries LLC

The Prayer of Freedom Group Study Workbook
(TPOF vs 4.3—260418, WB vs 1.1)
Author: Beatty Carmichael

This book is not intended to diagnose, treat, or replace professional medical, psychological, or therapeutic care. The author encourages readers to seek appropriate profession-al guidance when needed.

ISBN: 979-8-9890591-2-6

TABLE OF CONTENTS

Welcome p. 5

How to use this workbook p. 7

Leader's Quick Start Guide p. 8

Student Note Sheets

Session 1: Sin and Discipline (part 1) p. 15

Session 2: Sin and Discipline (part 2) p. 17

Session 3: A walk through the Bible (part 1) p. 23

Session 4: A walk through the Bible (part 2) p. 27

Session 5: Parable of the Unmerciful Servant p. 32

Session 6: Legal Rights p. 34

The Prayer of Freedom Book

Acknowledgements p. 40
Introduction p. 41
Prologue p. 43

Section 1—The Battle

Chapter 1: Ancient spiritual laws of discipline & breakthrough p. 51

Chapter 2: "Spiritual glasses" to see God's discipline p. 57

Chapter 3: How spirits of discipline work p. 63

Chapter 4: Parable of the Unmerciful Servant p. 67

Chapter 5: Three forms of "*basanizo*" discipline p. 71

Chapter 6: Legal Rights p. 77

Chapter 7: Sin is a cause for infirmity (Old Testament) p. 83

Chapter 8: Sin is a cause for infirmity (New Testament) **p. 89**

Chapter 9: Sin is still a cause for infirmity today **p. 93**

Chapter 10: Three types of "legal rights" **p. 97**

Section 2—Field Manual

Field Manual Introduction: **p. 109**

Chapter 11: The first steps to getting free **p. 113**

Chapter 12: Prayer of Freedom **p. 121**

Chapter 13: Helping others by "giving it forward" **p. 155**

Chapter 14: What to expect after completing the Prayer of Freedom **p. 163**

Chapter 15: Simple ways to help family and friends get freedom, too **p. 173**

Chapter 16: Your *next* step: help set your nation free **p. 177**

Chapter 17: Additional ways to grow and lead others **p. 181**

Chapter 18: About Get Radical Faith Ministries and how to help **p. 185**

Appendix

For Christian Friends **p. 191**

About the Author **p. 197**

Facilitator's Guide and Answer Key

Session 1 (Answer Key): Sin and Discipline (part 1) **p. 201**

Session 2 (Answer Key): Sin and Discipline (part 2) **p. 203**

Session 3 (Answer Key): A walk through the Bible (part 1) **p. 208**

Session 4 (Answer Key): A walk through the Bible (part 2) **p. 211**

Session 5 (Answer Key): Parable of the Unmerciful Servant **p. 215**

Session 6 (Answer Key): Legal Rights **p. 217**

Welcome

I'm really glad you have this workbook in your hands!

Whether you are joining a group study, leading one, or simply working through this on your own, my hope is the same: that what you discover here will not just inform you, but help bring real change to your life.

For many people, the struggles they carry have gone on so long they begin to feel normal. Sometimes it is chronic pain. Sometimes it is anxiety, fear, addiction, heaviness, relationship conflict, or patterns that never seem to fully go away. Often people have tried hard, prayed hard, read more, learned more—and still found themselves wondering why the problem remains.

That is why this workbook exists.

This study is designed to help you understand a simple but life-changing process for identifying and removing deeper spiritual roots that quietly keep many people stuck. And when the real root is addressed, the change can be surprising—in the best possible way.

Over the years, I have seen people who lived with fear and inner torment for years suddenly experience calm they had not felt since childhood. I have seen people battling addiction find that the cravings that ruled them simply lost their grip. I have seen long-standing pain leave so quickly that people stood there in tears, hardly able to believe what had just happened. And I have seen people carrying deep wounds from the past finally find freedom when they addressed the spiritual issue underneath it all.

That does not mean every story looks the same. And it does not mean this is about hype or emotional moments. It simply means there is real hope.

So, if part of you feels hopeful, but another part feels hesitant, that's completely normal. Anytime we begin looking beneath the surface of long-standing struggles, it can feel unfamiliar at first—and that's okay. My encouragement is simple: don't overthink your way out of this before you begin. Just walk through it. Let the process speak for itself.

Some of you are using this workbook as part of a group study. Others are working through it personally at your own pace. Both approaches work very well.

If you are going through this on your own, you can absolutely use the group study videos by yourself and complete the workbook step by step. Many people actually find this a very meaningful way to slow down, reflect, and apply what they are learning personally. Just be sure to read through the book sections included throughout this workbook as you go. The goal is not simply a momentary breakthrough, but learning a process you can continue using throughout your life—and confidently share with others.

In other words, this workbook is not only about getting free. It is also about learning how freedom works.

If you are a group study leader, I strongly encourage you to begin with the Leader's Guide section first. It will walk you through everything you need to lead with confidence, including practical instructions, teaching guidance, video access information, and completed answer pages. Starting there will make the study smoother and more effective for everyone involved.

However you are coming to this workbook, my prayer is that you will approach it with quiet expectation. Take your time. Be honest. Stay engaged. And most of all, keep going.

What you are about to learn has helped many people find freedom in places where they had nearly given up hope—and my hope is that it will do the same for you.

I'm honored to walk with you through it.

Beatty Carmichael

How to Use This Workbook

This workbook has been designed to make your group study simple and effective. Whether you are a facilitator leading a group or a participant joining one, everything you need is inside.

▶ If You Are a Group Leader

If you are leading a group, please turn to **The Leader's Guide and Answer Key** just after this section before beginning.

There you will find:

- Step-by-step instructions on **how to facilitate a group study**
- Suggestions for leading effective discussions
- Access information for the **group study videos**
- A brief **training video** on how to lead your group with confidence
- Complete worksheets **with answers filled** in to guide your teaching

Start there first. The Facilitator's Guide and Answer Key will give you everything you need to be fully prepared.

▶ If You Are a Participant

Simply use the **Student Note Sheets** section to follow along with the teaching videos and fill in your notes.

Leader's Quick Start Guide

Thank you for leading a Prayer of Freedom Group Study! This **six-session course** has been designed to make your role simple and effective. Here's how to get started:

1. Plan Your Group

- Decide when and how often your group will meet (for example: once a week for 6 weeks, or twice a week for 3 weeks).
- Each session will take about 60 minutes for the video teaching and discussion afterwards (plus optional fellowship time).
- Invite friends, family, or an existing study group you may be involved in.

Encourage each participant to purchase their own copy of *The Prayer of Freedom Group Study Workbook*. This is the same workbook you are holding now as the Leader, and it contains everything needed to fully participate in the study—note sheets at the beginning for following along with the videos, plus the complete *The Prayer of Freedom* book for doing the prayer portion and experiencing breakthrough.

In many regions, the printed workbook is the simplest and best option because it combines both the book and the worksheets in one place. However, in some parts of the world where printed copies are difficult to obtain or too expensive, participants may instead purchase the digital version of *The Prayer of Freedom* and download the worksheet pages separately from our website. The digital book is an essential part of the group study because participants will read key chapters as homework and personally go through the prayer process in Chapter 12, along with the follow-up chapters on how to stay free and help others experience freedom.

If your group is using the digital version of the book, either the group leader may download the worksheet pages and distribute them to participants, or participants may download them individually using the link provided. We strongly recommend printing the worksheets whenever possible, since participants are typically more attentive and engaged when they write notes on a paper copy as they follow along during the sessions. This approach allows groups in locations with limited access to printed books to still participate fully in the study at a much lower cost.

Workbooks can be ordered at: **ThePrayerOfFreedom.com/GroupStudy** (or directly on Amazon or other booksellers.)

The digital version of the worksheets can be found at the bottom of this page: **ThePrayerOfFreedom.com/GroupStudy-promo**.

2. Access the Videos

There are three ways to access and play the group study videos, depending on the device you prefer to use. They are screen casting them from our mobile app to your TV, playing them directly from YouTube on a smart TV, or playing them on your computer through our website.

Option 1: Screen Casting From Our Mobile App

Open the *Get Radical Faith mobile app*—the same app referenced in the book—tap *The Prayer of Freedom button*, then scroll to the bottom and select *Group Study Videos*. If your TV supports screen casting (such as Apple AirPlay or Android Screen Cast), you can mirror your phone or tablet screen to your TV so everyone can watch together. This option also allows translated versions of our videos to be selected within the video player when available.

▶ How to screencast from your phone to your TV

Screen casting (also called screen mirroring) is only available with smart TVs that support this feature. Here's how to screen cast from your phone:

If you are using an iPhone (Apple)
Swipe down from the top-right corner of your screen and tap **Screen Mirroring.** Then select your TV (or Apple TV) from the list. Once connected, anything on your phone—including the group study videos—will appear on your TV.

If you are using an Android phone
Swipe down from the top of your screen and tap **Screen Cast, Smart View, or Cast** (the name may vary by device). Then select your TV from the list. Your phone screen will appear on the TV so everyone can watch together.

If you don't see your TV listed, make sure your phone and TV are connected to the same Wi-Fi network. If needed, someone in your group may already be familiar with screen casting and can help set this up quickly.

Option 2: Play On Your Computer

You can also play the videos (and translated versions when available) on your computer by going to our website page: **https://ThePrayerOfFreedom.com/GroupStudyVideos**. Your group can either watch the videos on your computer, or if it is connected to a TV (for example, with an HDMI cable), you can this display it on your TV.

Option 3: Play Directly From YouTube

If your TV has the YouTube app, you can open YouTube and search for **PrayerOf FreedomGroupStudyVideos** (all one word, with no spaces) to locate our Group Study playlist. Open the playlist, then select the session you want to watch. (YouTube videos are in English only)

3. For the *First* Session

- Have each person write their name along the **outside edge** of their workbook (the rib of the book) so books don't get mixed up.
- Encourage participants to make their workbook unique—add a ribbon, bookmark, or colored mark so it's easy to spot.

4. Structure of Each Session

Each session lasts about one hour and includes two videos:

▶ **Watch Video 1: Teaching** (about 35-40 minutes) where Beatty introduces the session, then teaches it.

- Watch the teaching together.
- After the video, lead a **short discussion** (10-15 minutes) by asking 2–3 questions such as:
    - ***What stood out to you most from today's teaching?***
    - ***How does this connect with something in your own life?***
    - ***What is a takeaway or insight you want to remember from this session?***

- After the discussion, play the **Next Steps** video to close out the session

▶ **Watch Video 2: Next Steps** (5–10 minutes) where Beatty closes out the session and suggests the "next steps" homework assignment.

- Encourage participants to complete the assignment before the next session.

5. Create a Warm Environment

- Allow 15–20 minutes before starting for coffee, snacks, and fellowship.
- Keep the atmosphere relaxed and welcoming.
- Remind participants this is a safe space to share and grow.

6. For Sessions 5 and 6—IMPORTANT

Before wrapping up Sessions 5 and 6, take a moment to point your group to **Page 37** of this workbook. There, you'll find ways to **Multiply the Impact of Freedom**—through *Giving It Forward, Leading a Group Study*, and *Going Deeper with the Master Class.*

The purpose is simple: to help spread the message of repentance and healing to set as many people free as possible.

7. Register as a Group Study Leader

We'd love to stay connected with you as a Group Study Leader and keep you updated on new resources and opportunities with the Group Study program. This is a key part of how we're spreading the message, and we plan to build an encouraging network for facilitators — with community connections, additional training, and leadership opportunities. To register and stay plugged in, visit the link below:

ThePrayerofFreedom.com/GroupStudyVideos

Student Note Sheets

Session 1
Sin and Discipline (part 1)

Panorama of the full Master Class course

- **Session 1:** Sin and Discipline
- **Session 2:** What the Bible says about sin and consequence
- **Session 3:** Legal Rights in the spiritual realm
  (*Group study ends here*)

- **Session 4:** 3 Types of Legal Rights and how to get free
- **Session 5:** Covering and Authority
- **Session 6:** Success Tips and List Preparation Guide

Overview

__________ is a significant cause of sickness, infirmity, and all kinds of life issues

Not all illnesses are tied to sin... ...but many of the issues we deal with *are.*

- It's all part of God's plan to give you abundant life
- **John 10:10** (ESV) - "The thief comes to steal, kill, and destroy, but I came that [you] may have life, and have it abundantly."

Discipline vs Punishment

- Discipline is for ____________; punishment is for ____________.
- Discipline ______________________; punishment ______________________.

God's spiritual laws of _______________

- **Heb 12:4-6 (NIV) -** [4] In your struggle against sin, you have not yet resisted to the point of shedding your blood. [5] And have you completely forgotten this word of encouragement that addresses you as a father addresses his son? It says, "My son, do not make light of the Lord's discipline, and do not lose heart when he rebukes you, [6] because the Lord disciplines the one he loves, and he chastens everyone he accepts as his son."
- If you are his child, God *will* discipline you when you sin... even if you live a "righteous" life

>> Homework Assignment <<

- **BEFORE LEAVING CLASS**
  - Pray **The Simplified Prayer** (at beginning of Part 2 Field Manual)
  - Download the "Get Radical Faith" mobile app (from your app store)
  - Select two **Prayer Buddies** to pray for you while going through the Prayer of Freedom (have them pray the "Beginning Prayer" on your behalf... found in Chapter 12)

- **ON YOUR OWN FROM HOME**
  - Read Chapter 11 and do the Issue Grid
  - **Do Chapter 12 List Preparation Guide →** complete List Preparation Guide before Session 2
  - (as time allows: begin reading *The Prayer of Freedom* book, Part 1)

Session 2:
Sin and Discipline (part 2)

The ___________ realm

- This is where God's discipline occurs

- **Eph 6:12 (ESV) -** For we do not wrestle against flesh and blood, but against the rulers, against the authorities, against the cosmic powers over this present darkness, against the spiritual forces of evil in the heavenly places.
- **TLB version: -** For we are not fighting against people made of flesh and blood, <u>but against persons without bodies</u>...

PERSONS WITHOUT BODIES...

▸ **___________ spirits**

- **Holy Spirit - Gen 1:1-2 (ESV) -** [1] In the beginning, God created the heavens and the earth. [2] The earth was without form and void, and darkness was over the face of the deep. And the <u>Spirit of God</u> was hovering over the face of the waters.
- **Angels** -- spirit beings, and they are also "persons"
- **Spirit of <u>skill</u>** - **Exo 28:3 (ESV)** - You shall speak to all the skillful, whom I have filled with a <u>spirit of skill</u>, that they make Aaron's garments to consecrate him for my priesthood.
- **Spirit of <u>wisdom</u> - Deu 34:9 (ESV) -** And Joshua the son of Nun was full of the <u>spirit of wisdom</u>, for Moses had laid his hands on him. So the people of Israel obeyed him and did as the LORD had commanded Moses.
- **Spirit of <u>truth</u> - Joh 16:13 (ESV) -** When the <u>Spirit of truth</u> comes, he will guide you into all the truth, for he will not speak on his own authority, but whatever he hears he will speak, and he will declare to you the things that are to come.

- **Spirit of gentleness - 1 Cor 4:21 (ESV) -** What do you wish? Shall I come to you with a rod, or with love in a spirit of gentleness?

▶ ____________ spirits

- **Spirit of jealousy - Num 5:14 (ESV) -** and if the spirit of jealousy comes over him and he is jealous of his wife who has defiled herself, or if the spirit of jealousy comes over him and he is jealous of his wife, though she has not defiled herself
- **Spirit of terror - 1 Sam 16:14 (ESV) -** Now the Spirit of the LORD departed from Saul, and a harmful spirit from the LORD tormented him.
- **Spirit of lying - 1 Kings 22:21-22 (ESV) -** [21] Then a spirit came forward and stood before the LORD, saying, 'I will entice him.' [22] And the LORD said to him, 'By what means?' And he said, 'I will go out, and will be a lying spirit in the mouth of all his prophets.' And he said, 'You are to entice him, and you shall succeed; go out and do so.'
- **Spirit of confusion - Isai 19:14 (ESV) -** The LORD has mingled within her a spirit of confusion, and they will make Egypt stagger in all its deeds, as a drunken man staggers in his vomit.
- **Spirit of whoredom - Hos 4:12 (ESV) -** My people inquire of a piece of wood, and their walking staff gives them oracles. For a spirit of whoredom has led them astray, and they have left their God to play the whore.
- **Spirit of divination - Act 16:16 (ESV) -** As we were going to the place of prayer, we were met by a slave girl who had a spirit of divination and brought her owners much gain by fortune-telling.
- **Spirit of fear - 2 Tim 1:7 (NASB) -** For God has not given us a spirit of fear, but of power and of love and of a sound mind.

▸ Additional __________ spirits (not referenced in Bible)

- Spirit of <u>addiction</u>
- Spirit of <u>depression</u>
- Spirit of <u>heaviness</u>
- Spirit of <u>anger</u>
- Spirit of <u>violence</u>
- Spirit of <u>pain</u>
- Spirit of <u>suicide</u>

▸ ____________ spirits

- **Spirit of <u>muteness and seizures</u> - Mar 9:17-18 (ESV) -** [17]
  And someone from the crowd answered him, "Teacher, I
  brought my son to you, for he has a <u>spirit</u> that makes him <u>mute</u>.
  [18] And whenever it <u>seizes him</u>, it throws him down, and he
  foams and grinds his teeth and becomes rigid. So I asked your
  disciples to cast it out, and they were not able."
- **Spirit of <u>Fever</u> - Luk 4:38-39 (ESV) -** [38] Jesus left the synagogue and went to the home of Simon. Now Simon's mother-in-law was suffering from a high fever, and they asked
  Jesus to help her. [39] So he bent over her and <u>rebuked the fever</u>, and it left her. She got up at once and began to wait on them.
- **Spirit of "<u>Bent Spine Syndrome</u>"** (camptocormia) - **Luk 13:10-11 (ESV)** - [10] On a Sabbath Jesus was teaching in one of
  the synagogues, [11] and a woman was there who had been <u>crippled by a spirit</u> for eighteen years. She was bent over and could not straighten up at all.

- Many spirits are ____________ - they amplify a specific characteristic

Sin, discipline and repentance

- **The 5 Step Process of Man**

(1) ___________ made in God's image

- **Gen 1:27 (ESV)** - So God created man in his own image, in the image of God he created him; male and female he created them.

(2) Man ___________

- **Gen 3:6-7a (NIV)** - [6] When the woman saw that the fruit of the tree [*of the knowledge of good and evil*] was good for food and pleasing to the eye, and also desirable for gaining wisdom, she took some and ate it. She also gave some to her husband, who was with her, and he ate it. [7] Then the eyes of both of them were opened...

(3) ___________lost God's image

- **Gen 5:3 (ESV)** - When Adam had lived 130 years, he fathered a son <u>in *his* own likeness</u>, after his image, and named him Seth.

(4) ___________made in God's image

- **Rom 8:3 (ESV)** - For what the Law could not do, weak as it was through the flesh, God did: <u>sending His own Son in the likeness of sinful flesh</u> and as an offering for sin, He condemned sin in the flesh
- **Heb 1:3a (ESV)** - He is the radiance of the glory of God and the <u>exact imprint of his nature</u>, and he upholds the universe by the word of his power...

- **We are to be conformed to Jesus's image ... *God's* image**
- **Rom 8:29 (ESV) -** For those whom he foreknew he also predestined to be conformed to the image of his Son, in order that he might be the firstborn among many brothers

- **Question:** How do we conform to the image of his Son?
- **Answer:** _______________ of our sin

(5) Man ____________ to restore God's image

- When we repent of our sin, it removes the sin
  --> this was Jesus's primary message

- **_______________ is the primary message throughout the Bible**
  - **God in OT --> Joel 2:12-13 (ESV) -** [12] "Yet even now," declares the LORD, "return to me with all your heart ["repent"], with fasting, with weeping, and with mourning; [13] and rend your hearts and not your garments." Return to the LORD your God, for he is gracious and merciful, slow to anger, and abounding in steadfast love; and he relents over disaster.
  - **John the Baptist --> Mat 3:1-2 (ESV) -** In those days John the Baptist came preaching in the wilderness of Judea, [2] "Repent, for the kingdom of heaven is at hand."
  - **Jesus --> Mat 4:17 (ESV) -** From that time Jesus began to preach, saying, "Repent, for the kingdom of heaven is at hand."

- **Sin does two things**

1. breaks ____________with God

→ to restore: repent of sins ____________

2. breaks ____________ of God

→ to restore: repent of sins ____________

- **God and Michelangelo - a picture of what this looks like**
- God conform us back to his image in the same way Michelangelo created beautiful sculptures --> one chip at a time
- **Luk 6:40 (ESV)** - A disciple is not above his teacher, but everyone when he is fully trained will be like his teacher.

>> Homework Assignment <<

- **ON YOUR OWN FROM HOME**
  - **Begin doing Prayers 1, 2 and 3** (second half of Chapter 12)
  - (finish List Preparation Guide if not already completed)
  - (continue reading through *The Prayer of Freedom* Part 1)

Session 3:
A walk through the Bible (OT)

Spiritual laws vs God's ________

- Many of God's spiritual laws operate *outside* of his covenants with man

- **Example 1 Seventh Day:** God declared the seventh day ________

- **Example 2 Tithe:** God declares the tithe ("a 10th part") is ________

- **God's spiritual laws of sin and discipline are the ________**

- **Malachi 3:6 (NIV) -** "I the LORD do not change...
- **James 1:17 (NIV) -** Every good and perfect gift is from above, coming down from the Father of the heavenly lights, who does not change...

A walk through the Bible - sin and ________

OLD TESTAMENT

- **(1) Miriam and leprosy: Num 12:1-10** (NIV) - 1 Miriam and Aaron began to talk against Moses because of his Cushite wife, for he had married a Cushite. 2 "Has the LORD spoken only through Moses?" they asked. "Hasn't he also spoken through us?" And the LORD heard this. 3 (Now Moses was a very humble man, more humble than anyone else on the face of the earth.) 4 At once the LORD said to Moses, Aaron and Miriam, "Come out to the tent of meeting, all three of you." So the three of them went out. 5 Then the LORD came down in a pillar of cloud; he stood at the entrance to the tent and summoned Aaron and Miriam. When the two of them stepped forward, 6 he said, "Listen to my words: "When there is a prophet among you, I, the LORD, reveal myself to them in visions, I speak to them in dreams. 7 But this is not true of my servant Moses; he is faithful in all my house. 8 With him I speak face to face, clearly and not in riddles; he sees the form of the LORD. <u>Why then were you not afraid to speak against my servant Moses</u>?" 9 The anger of the LORD burned against them, and he left them. 10 When the cloud lifted from above the tent, <u>Miriam's skin was leprous</u>—it became as white as snow...

- **(2) Venomous snakes: Num 21:4-7a (NIV) -** 4 "They traveled from Mount Hor ... but the people grew impatient on the way; 5 they spoke against God... 6 Then the LORD sent <u>venomous snakes</u> among them; they bit the people and many Israelites died. 7 The people came to Moses and said, '<u>We sinned</u> when we spoke against the LORD ...'"

- **(3) Life of lack: Deu 28:15-20 (NIV) -** 15 However, if you <u>do not obey the LORD your God</u> and do not carefully follow all his commands and decrees I am giving you today, <u>all these curses will come on you and overtake you</u>: 16 You will be cursed in the city and cursed in the country. 17 Your basket and your kneading trough will be cursed. 18 The fruit of your womb will be cursed, and the crops of your land, and the calves of your herds and the lambs of your flocks. 19 You will be cursed when you come in and cursed when you go out. 20 The LORD will send on you curses, confusion and rebuke in everything you put your hand to...

- **(4) Diseases of Egypt: Deu 28:58-61 (NIV)** - [58] "If you do not carefully follow all the words of this law, which are written in this book, and do not revere this glorious and awesome name —the LORD your God— [59] the LORD will send fearful plagues on you and your descendants, harsh and prolonged disasters, and severe and lingering illnesses. [60] He will bring on you all the diseases of Egypt that you dreaded, and they will cling to you. [61] The LORD will also bring on you every kind of sickness and disaster not recorded in this Book of the Law..."

- **(5) Jeroboam's hand shrivels: 1 Kings 13:1-4 (NIV)** - [1] By the word of the LORD a man of God came from Judah to Bethel, as Jeroboam was standing by the altar to make an offering. [2] By the word of the LORD he cried out against the altar: "Altar, altar! This is what the LORD says: 'A son named Josiah will be born to the house of David. On you he will sacrifice the priests of the high places who make offerings here, and human bones will be burned on you.'" [3] That same day the man of God gave a sign: "This is the sign the LORD has declared: The altar will be split apart and the ashes on it will be poured out." [4] When King Jeroboam heard what the man of God cried out against the altar at Bethel, he stretched out his hand from the altar and said, "Seize him!" But the hand he stretched out toward the man shriveled up, so that he could not pull it back.

- **(6) Gehazi and leprosy: 2 Kings 5:14-27 (NIV)** - [14] So [Naaman, the Syrian] went down and dipped himself in the Jordan seven times, as [Elisha] the man of God had told him, and his flesh was restored and became clean like that of a young boy. [15] Then Naaman and all his attendants went back to the man of God . He stood before him and said, "Now I know that there is no God in all the world except in Israel. So please accept a gift from your servant." [16] The prophet answered, "As surely as the LORD lives, whom I serve, I will not accept a thing." And even though Naaman urged him, he refused... [*Naaman leaves and goes a short way*]... [21] So Gehazi [Elisha's servant] hurried after Naaman. When Naaman saw him running toward him, he got down from the chariot to meet him. "Is everything all right?" he asked. [22] "Everything is all right," Gehazi answered. "My master sent me to say, 'Two young men from the company of the prophets have just come to me from the hill country of Ephraim. Please give them a talent of silver and two sets of clothing.'" [23] "By all means, take two talents," said Naaman. He urged Gehazi to accept them, and then tied up the two talents of silver in two bags, with two sets of clothing. He gave them to two of his servants, and they carried them ahead of Gehazi. [24] When Gehazi came to the hill, he took the things from the servants and put them away in the house. He sent the men away and they left. 25 When he went in and stood before his master, Elisha asked him, "Where have you been, Gehazi?" "Your servant didn't go anywhere," Gehazi answered. 26 But Elisha said to him, "Was not my spirit with you when the man got down from his chariot to meet you? Is this the time to take money or to accept clothes—or olive groves and vineyards, or flocks and herds, or male and female slaves? 27 Naaman's leprosy will cling to you and to your descendants forever." Then Gehazi went from Elisha's presence and his skin was leprous—it had become as white as snow.

- **(7) Uzziah and leprosy: 2 Chr 26:16-21 (NIV) -** 16 But after Uzziah became powerful, his pride led to his downfall. He was unfaithful to the LORD his God, and entered the temple of the LORD to burn incense on the altar of incense. 17 Azariah the priest with eighty other courageous priests of the LORD followed him in. 18 They confronted King Uzziah and said, "It is not right for you, Uzziah, to burn incense to the LORD. That is for the priests, the descendants of Aaron, who have been consecrated to burn incense. Leave the sanctuary, for you have been unfaithful; and you will not be honored by the LORD God." 19 Uzziah, who had a censer in his hand ready to burn incense, became angry. While he was raging at the priests in their presence before the incense altar in the LORD's temple, leprosy broke out on his forehead. 20 When Azariah the chief priest and all the other priests looked at him, they saw that he had leprosy on his forehead, so they hurried him out. Indeed, he himself was eager to leave, because the LORD had afflicted him. 21 King Uzziah had leprosy until the day he died. He lived in a separate house —leprous, and banned from the temple of the LORD...

- **(8) King David infirmed: Psalms 32:1-4 (NLT) -** 1 Oh, what joy for those whose disobedience is forgiven, whose sin is put out of sight! 2 Yes, what joy for those whose record the LORD has cleared of guilt, whose lives are lived in complete honesty! 3 When I refused to confess my sin, my body wasted away, and I groaned all day long. 4 Day and night your hand of discipline was heavy on me. My strength evaporated like water in the summer heat.

>> Homework Assignment <<

- **Continue Prayers 1, 2 and 3** (second half of Chapter 12)
- (continue reading through *The Prayer of Freedom* Part 1)

Session 4:
A walk through the Bible (NT)

<u>NEW TESTAMENT</u>

- **(9) Woman with spirit of infirmity: Luk 13:10-13 (NIV)** - On a Sabbath Jesus was teaching in one of the synagogues, and a woman was there who had been crippled by a spirit for eighteen years. She was bent over and could not straighten up at all. When Jesus saw her, he called her forward and said to her, "Woman, you are set free from your infirmity." Then he put his hands on her, and immediately she straightened up and praised God.

    - It was due to sin -- how do we know? ...

    - Why did Jesus tell this man, "Sin no more, that nothing worse may happen to you?"

      Luk 13:14-16 (NIV) - [14] Indignant because Jesus had healed on the Sabbath, the synagogue leader said to the people, "There are six days for work. So come and be healed on those days, not on the Sabbath." [15] The Lord answered him, "You hypocrites! Doesn't each of you on the Sabbath untie your ox or donkey from the stall and lead it out to give it water? [16] Then should not this woman, a daughter of Abraham, <u>whom Satan has kept bound</u> for eighteen long years, be set free on the Sabbath day from what bound her?"

- **(10) Lame man at the pool: Joh 5:2-9,14 (ESV)** - [2] "Now there is in Jerusalem by the Sheep Gate a pool, in Aramaic called Bethesda, which has five roofed colonnades. [3] In these lay a multitude of invalids—blind, lame, and paralyzed. [5] One man was there who had been an invalid for thirty-eight years. [6] When Jesus saw him lying there and knew that he had already been there a long time... [8] Jesus said to him, 'Get up, take up your bed, and walk.' [9] And at once the man was healed, and he took up his bed and walked.... [14] Afterward Jesus found him in the temple and said to him, 'See, you are well! <u>Sin no more, that nothing worse may happen to you</u>.'"

    - **Question:** Why did Jesus tell this man, "Sin no more, that nothing worse may happen to you?

- **Answer:** because ___________ can be a root of infirmity

- **(11) Herod Agrippa: Act 12:21-23 (NIV)** - [21] On the appointed day Herod, wearing his royal robes, sat on his throne and delivered a public address to the people. [22] They shouted, "This is the voice of a god, not of a man." [23] Immediately, because Herod did not give praise to God, an angel of the Lord struck him down, and he was eaten by worms and died.

- **(12) Ananias lies to God: Acts 5:1-5 (NIV)** - [1] Now a man named Ananias, together with his wife Sapphira, also sold a piece of property. [2] With his wife's full knowledge he kept back part of the money for himself, but brought the rest and put it at the apostles' feet. [3] Then Peter said, "Ananias, how is it that Satan has so filled your heart that you have lied to the Holy Spirit and have kept for yourself some of the money you received for the land? [4] Didn't it belong to you before it was sold? And after it was sold, wasn't the money at your disposal? What made you think of doing such a thing? You have not lied just to human beings but to God." [5] When Ananias heard this, he fell down and died. And great fear seized all who heard what had happened.

- **(13) Man with father's wife: 1 Corinthians 5:1-5 (NIV)** - [1] It is actually reported that there is sexual immorality among you, and of a kind that even pagans do not tolerate: A man is sleeping with his father's wife. [2] And you are proud! Shouldn't you rather have gone into mourning and have put out of your fellowship the man who has been doing this? [3] For my part, even though I am not physically present, I am with you in spirit. As one who is present with you in this way, I have already passed judgment in the name of our Lord Jesus on the one who has been doing this. [4] So when you are assembled and I am with you in spirit, and the power of our Lord Jesus is present, [5] hand this man over to Satan for the destruction of the flesh, so that his spirit may be saved on the day of the Lord.

- **(14) Lord's supper: 1 Cor 11:29-30 (NIV)** - [29] "For those who eat and drink without discerning the body of Christ eat and drink judgment on themselves. [30] That is why many among you are weak and sick, and a number of you have fallen asleep."

- **1 Cor 11:32 (NIV)** - "... when we are judged in this way by the Lord, we are being **disciplined** so that we will not be finally condemned with the world."

- **(15) Call for the elders: Jam 5:14-16 (ESV)** - [14] "Is anyone among you sick? Let him call for the elders of the church, and let them pray over him, anointing him with oil in the name of the Lord. [15]
And the prayer of faith will save the one who is sick, and the Lord will raise him up. And if he has committed sins, he will be forgiven. [16]
Therefore, confess your sins to one another... that you may be healed. The prayer of a righteous person has great power as it is working."

___________vs Sin

- **Not all sickness is due to sin** --> some can come from ______________ causes

- **What about the blind man?**
  - **Joh 9:1-3 (NIV)** - [1] As he went along, he saw a man blind from birth. [2] His disciples asked him, "Rabbi, who sinned, this man or his parents, that he was born blind?" [3]
"Neither this man nor his parents sinned," said Jesus, "but this happened so that the works of God might be displayed in him.

- **What if you've lived a sinful life and have lots of issues?**
  - **Isaiah 46:12-13 (NLT)** - "Listen to me, you stubborn people who are so far from doing right. For I am ready to set things right, not in the distant future, but right now! I am ready to save Jerusalem and show my glory to Israel.

Healing vs _________ will

- **1 Joh 5:14-15 (NIV) -** [14] This is the confidence we have in approaching God: that if we ask anything according to his will, he hears us. [15] And if we know that he hears us—whatever we ask—we know that we have what we asked of him.

- **2 Pet 3:9 (NIV) -** The Lord is not slow in keeping his promise, as some understand slowness. Instead he is patient with you, not wanting anyone to perish, but everyone to come to repentance.

Conclusion

- God's word is clear -- our sins produce earthly consequences
- **Joh 10:10 (ESV) -** "The thief comes only to steal and kill and destroy. I came that they may have life and have it abundantly."

Question: How do you get that abundant life?

Answer: By ____________ of your sin

- **Mal 3:6-12 (NIV) -** [6] "I the LORD do not change. So you, the
descendants of Jacob, are not destroyed. [7] Ever since the time of
your ancestors you have turned away from my decrees and
have not kept them. Return to me, and I will return to you," says
the LORD Almighty. "But you ask, 'How are we to return?' [8]
"Will a mere mortal rob God? Yet you rob me. "But you ask,
'How are we robbing you?' "In tithes and offerings. [9] You are
under a curse —your whole nation—because you are robbing
me. [10] Bring the whole tithe into the storehouse, that there may
be food in my house. Test me in this," says the LORD Almighty,
"and see if I will not throw open the floodgates of heaven and
pour out so much blessing that there will not be room enough
to store it. [11] I will prevent pests from devouring your crops,
and the vines in your fields will not drop their fruit before it is

ripe, " says the LORD Almighty. 12 "Then all the nations will call you blessed, for yours will be a delightful land," says the LORD Almighty.

- When you ____________ from sin, God promises the discipline will be stopped and ____________ will be restored

>> Homework Assignment <<

- **Continue Prayers 1, 2 and 3** (second half of Chapter 12)
- (continue reading through *The Prayer of Freedom* Part 1)

Session 5:
Parable of the Unmerciful Servant

Isn't ________ good for us?

- **2 types of suffering**
    - Disobedience --> discipline -- YES stop
    - Obedience --> persecution -- NO stop

Parable of the ________ Servant

Mat 18:21-35 (NIV) -

[21] Then Peter came to Jesus and asked, "Lord, how many times shall
I forgive my brother or sister who sins against me? Up to seven
times?" [22] Jesus answered, "I tell you, not seven times, but seventy-
seven times.

[23] "Therefore, the kingdom of heaven is like a king who wanted to
settle accounts with his servants. [24] As he began the settlement, a
man who owed him ten thousand bags of gold was brought to him.
[25] Since he was not able to pay, the master ordered that he and his
wife and his children and all that he had be sold to repay the debt. [26]
"At this the servant fell on his knees before him. 'Be patient with
me,' he begged, 'and I will pay back everything.' [27] The servant's
master took pity on him, canceled the debt and let him go.

[28] "But when that servant went out, he found one of his fellow
servants who owed him a hundred silver coins. He grabbed him and
began to choke him. 'Pay back what you owe me!' he demanded. [29]
"His fellow servant fell to his knees and begged him, 'Be patient
with me, and I will pay it back.' [30] "But he refused. Instead, he went
off and had the man thrown into prison until he could pay the debt.

[31] When the other servants saw what had happened, they were outraged and went and told their master everything that had happened. [32] "Then the master called the servant in. 'You wicked servant,' he said, 'I canceled all that debt of yours because you begged me to. [33] Shouldn't you have had mercy on your fellow servant just as I had on you?' [34] In anger his master handed him over to the jailers to be **tortured**, until he should pay back all he owed.

[35] "This is how my heavenly Father **will** treat each of you unless you forgive your brother or sister from your heart."

- **Greek for "torturer"** (also translated as "jailer") -- means "one who elicits the truth by the use of the rack"
    - Root "_______________" meaning: **to torture** -- pain, toil, torment

(1) Mat 8:5-6 - When he had entered Capernaum, a centurion came forward to him, appealing to him, "Lord, my servant is lying paralyzed at home, <u>suffering</u> terribly." -- **physical suffering**

(2) 2 Pet 2:7-8 - and if he rescued righteous Lot, greatly distressed by the sensual conduct of the wicked (for as that righteous man lived among them day after day, he was <u>tormenting</u> his righteous soul over their lawless deeds that he saw and heard) -- **mental suffering**

(3) Rev 12:2 - She was pregnant and was crying out in birth pains and the <u>agony</u> of giving birth -- **physical pain**

Session 6:
Legal Rights

A practical look at ________ warfare

- **Eph 6:12 (ESV)** - For we do not wrestle against flesh and blood, but against the rulers, against the authorities, against the cosmic powers over this present darkness, against the spiritual forces of evil in the heavenly places.
  - **Eph 6:12 (TLB)** - For we are not fighting against people made of flesh and blood, but against persons without bodies...

Legal ________ is part of God's design

- **Eph 1:20-21 (ESV)** - " [20] ...when [God] raised him [Jesus] from the dead and seated him at his right hand in the heavenly places, [21] far above all rule and authority and power and dominion, and above every name that is named..."
- **Mat 28:18 (ESV)** - "And Jesus came and said to them, "All authority in heaven and on earth has been given to me.'"
- **Job 1:6 (ESV)** - "Now there was a day when the sons of God came to present themselves before the LORD, and Satan also came among them"
- **Heb 12:22-24 (ESV)** - "[22] But you have come to Mount Zion and to the city of the living God, the heavenly Jerusalem, and to innumerable angels in festal gathering, [23] and to the assembly of the firstborn who are enrolled in heaven, and to God, the judge of all, and to the spirits of the righteous made perfect, [24] and to Jesus, the mediator of a new covenant, and to the sprinkled blood that speaks a better word than the blood of Abel"

Unrepented Sins and Legal Rights

4 Steps of a Deliverance

1. ______________________________

2. ______________________________

3. ______________________________

4. ______________________________

Evidence of __________ __________ in scripture

- **Col 2:13c-15 (ESV) -** " [13] ... [Jesus] having forgiven us all our trespasses, [14] by canceling the record of debt that stood against us with its legal demands. This he set aside, nailing it to the cross. [15] He disarmed the rulers and authorities and put them to open shame, by triumphing over them in him."

What spiritual attacks look like

[Diagram]

Act 3:19 (NIV) - "Repent, then, and turn to God, so that your sins may be wiped out, that times of refreshing may come from the Lord"

- repenting of sins brings refreshing times now

Multiply the Impact of Freedom

1. Give It Forward

One of the simplest and most powerful ways to extend the impact of *The Prayer of Freedom* is to give it forward. Keep a few extra copies of the book on hand—whether at home, in your car, or at work—so when God places someone in your path, you're ready to share. A book freely given often becomes the spark of freedom for someone else. To learn more about how to make this part of your personal ministry, see **Chapter 13**.

2. Lead a Group Study

You've just experienced the power of walking through this process together—why not host your own group? You don't need to be a teacher or expert; the videos and workbook do the teaching for you. All it takes is inviting a few friends, creating a welcoming space, and letting God do the rest. To learn how to become a Group Study Facilitator and lead your own group, visit the link below:

ThePrayerOfFreedom.com/GroupStudy

3. Go Deeper with the Master Class

If you're ready to go beyond the basics and dive deeper into the principles of freedom, the Master Class is your next step. This 13-session, in-depth course unpacks spiritual laws in greater detail, equips you with advanced applications, and gives you the confidence to help others walk through this process effectively. To learn more about joining the Master Class, visit the link below.

ThePrayerOfFreedom.com/MasterClass

Become a Group Study Leader

If you've experienced the breakthroughs of *The Prayer of Freedom* and want to help others experience the same, that's exactly what the Group Study is all about. As a leader, you don't need to be a teacher or an expert—the videos and workbook do the teaching for you. Your role is simply to invite a few friends, create a welcoming space, and watch as lives begin to change.

Becoming a Group Study Leader and leading your own group is easier than you think, and it's one of the most rewarding ways to share this message of freedom with others. To learn how to get started, just visit the link below. There you'll find a short video that walks you through everything you need to begin leading your own group..

ThePrayerOfFreedom.com/GroupStudy

The Prayer of Freedom Book

ACKNOWLEDGMENTS

This book was born of a passion to serve God and set his people free. It would not have been possible were it not for a number of people who were instrumental in helping bring this book to reality.

First is **my wife, PA,** who helped me these last seven years as God trained and instructed me in the precepts behind the Prayer of Freedom.

Second is **Eric Schrag**, my editor, without whom this book would not be the amazing work that it is. It carries his "DNA" as much as it does mine, and it was his tireless efforts that make it so easy to understand.

Third is **Phyllis Tarbox** of Above and Beyond Christian Counseling, who greatly clarified many technical aspects pertaining to this subject. She also shared a systematic approach of prayers to God that ultimately led to the Prayer of Freedom.

Fourth is **Ken Fish** of Orbis Ministries. Though we've never officially met, his teachings related to "agreement sins" (my term) and secret societies were influential in making a critical portion of this prayer possible.

And fifth is a host of others, including **Father Spotswood** and **Sydney Petite**, who helped bring into sharper focus many aspects instrumental in setting people free.

To all of you, I thank God that he brought you into my life, and I thank you for your crucial contributions to this work!

INTRODUCTION

(***Author's note:*** *if you haven't already scanned the QR code on the front cover to watch my short video, I encourage you to do so before continuing*)

Rob and Lilly had been fighting in their marriage for ten years and were always at each other's throats. Even after five years of marriage counseling, they still fought every day. Things kept happening that would instantly "trigger" them into yelling and fighting.

But as soon as they applied the Prayer of Freedom to their lives, everything changed. They went from bickering and arguing every day to peace and calm in their home for the first time in years.

Rob said it is the most peaceful time they have *ever* had in their marriage. He said, "Both Lilly and I changed overnight. There is an overwhelming sense of peace in both of us that we have never experienced before. We've started doing things we had never been able to do together—preparing dinner together, eating meals together, cleaning up together. We're now talking and having fun just being a husband and wife rather than fighting all the time. I can't believe the difference it's made and how *quickly* it happened!"

So, what *did* happen? What's the secret behind the Prayer of Freedom?

The secret lies in understanding why prayer seems to work at some times and not at others—and how prayer works when it aligns with the spiritual laws that govern the unseen realm.

Think about it. Most people believe in some form of Higher Power, pure Love, or Creator. So, for simplicity, I'll call this 'God,' as the one who created everything. And if he created everything, wouldn't *he* have power to fix our problems?

Of course he would!

And if you're like most people, when problems get big enough you will eventually cry out to God for help and ask him to fix those problems. Yet, for a lot of people, it seems he doesn't answer their prayers at all, so why bother?

I get it! I used to be that way myself.

Then I discovered specific, spiritual laws that, when we apply them, our prayers more often get answered.

And if you've been praying and nothing has changed yet, that doesn't mean something is wrong with you—it may simply mean no one ever explained how these laws work.

How do I know? Because once I began applying them—and teaching others how to do the same—I began seeing prayers answered far more consistently than I ever thought possible!

For example, just a few days ago as I'm writing this, I taught this approach to a woman named Whitney who had been suffering from chronic pain for years. The doctors had been treating her symptoms for a long time, but the source of her pain had been misdiagnosed—it wasn't medical at all. She prayed to God using this approach and asked him to heal her pain. When I followed up with her a few days later she texted me back, saying, "It worked! My hips have not hurt and my sciatic pain down my back is gone too! My big toe feels much better. My neck pain and tension in my shoulders went away and I have felt so much more relaxed! Thank you very much!"

So, as you go through this book, I'll show you what I've learned about these laws and how to apply them in your life to get *your* prayers for healing or restoration answered, too!

To illustrate how powerful this approach is, let me share a survey I did...

I volunteer teach at an addiction recovery center. While preparing to write this book, I wanted to statistically measure how effective these laws were, so I did a survey with my students. This wasn't a clinical study—just a simple, honest way to measure what happened when people actually completed the process.

As you might imagine, most of them were dealing with many issues in their lives—all kinds of **personal issues** (*anger, shame, broken relationships, constant sickness*); **chronic pain** (*arthritis, muscle pain, degenerative discs, lupus*); **mental problems** (*depression, bipolar disorder, anxiety, voices in their heads*); **addiction urges** (*for cigarettes, drugs, alcohol, pornography, and sex*); and much more.

I had each student list the problems they were dealing with, rate how intense each one was, and then do the Prayer of Freedom. Of those who completed it, here's what happened...

Nearly 9 out of every 10 students saw almost all their issues *completely* disappear—**100% relief** of chronic pain, depression, anxiety, addictions, anger, and all their other issues! All of it... *gone!*

And for the few who still had remaining issues, the intensity of those issues had decreased to one-third of their original level.

And on a broader scale, by guiding people through the Prayer of Freedom, I've seen diabetes disappear within 5 months. I see arthritis, glaucoma and sleep apnea vanish in less than 24 hours. I see marriage relationships restored. I see depression, anxiety, and addictions completely melt away. I see bipolar disorder, restless leg syndrome, and allergies vanish. And a lot more!

Not every story looks the same, but the pattern is consistent.

In the following pages I share many stories of people who applied the Prayer of Freedom in their lives. Their stories seem unbelievable until you understand how these laws actually work. And while their stories might sound "too good to be true," I assure you they are all real, though I've changed the names to protect their privacy.

PROLOGUE

One day at Walmart I met a pastor in the grocery aisle. As we talked, he shared how he had lost most of the vision in his left eye due to a stroke.

I asked if I could pray for him. He said, "I just came back from a prayer meeting at church where everyone prayed for me. Nothing happened—I can still barely see out of that eye."

I told him, "That's okay. I've learned things that have made my prayers far more consistently answered than they used to be. May I try?"

He agreed, so I prayed for him.

Within *five minutes* his vision was restored to about 80% perfect!

I share this story for two reasons. First, to encourage you that if you've been praying for healing or freedom from problems or conflicts without results, don't lose hope! There is still a solution. Second, to show what's possible when you follow God's spiritual laws for receiving answered prayer.

To be perfectly honest, I'm nothing special. I don't have a special gift of prayer or anything like that. Anyone can do what I did because it wasn't *me* who did it.

What I've come to understand is there are spiritual laws that impact our prayers, yet most of us know nothing about them. But once you learn how to apply these laws, you'll see God answer many of your prayers for healing and restoration quickly. I know, because it's happened to me and almost everyone I've taught.

Before we go any further, I want to give a simple perspective to help guide how you approach what you're about to read. In life, people often work from patterns they may not fully understand, yet those patterns still prove useful because they consistently create the desired results.

An example is a farmer. He can't fully explain what happens beneath the soil, but he understands the pattern—when he plants seed and the conditions are right, growth follows. He doesn't need to understand how all of it works because the pattern consistently proves itself when it produces a harvest.

What I'm describing in this book works in a similar way. Over years of working with people facing chronic pain, emotional struggles, and more, I began noticing patterns that repeated themselves again and again. As people followed the process I outline in this book, freedom almost always followed. They didn't have to understand how everything worked—the pattern proved itself by the results it produced.

Because of that, you don't have to understand everything yourself. Simply pay attention to what happens when you apply what you're about to learn. And if it brings freedom to you or a loved one, then it's doing exactly what it's meant to do.

Why aren't your prayers being answered?

As we begin, the first thing I want to talk about is *the spiritual laws of praying to God.*

If you're suffering with a persistent problem—a mental, emotional, or physical issue like relationship conflicts, depression, anger, arthritis, or anything else—and you want freedom but nothing has worked, believe me, you're not alone.

If you've felt in your heart there is a God who created you and everything you see, then you probably believe he has the power to heal you and remove that problem. So, perhaps you've prayed to him, hoping he would answer your prayers and set you free.

If that is you, the fact that you're reading this book right now most likely means he *hasn't* answered those prayers yet. Which brings us to the BIG question: "Why do some prayers seem to work... while others don't?"

And that's what I've discovered—specific, spiritual laws that play a significant role in our lives. Let me explain...

In our world, physical laws govern everything we experience: gravity makes things fall, water freezes into ice, and fire turns wood to ash. Yet, while these laws shape our physical world, they cannot solve the personal challenges we desperately want freedom from.

Similarly, just as physical laws govern our physical world, spiritual laws govern our personal challenges. And by applying certain spiritual laws, I've seen people get free from most of those problems within days... literally!

What's ultimately going on is many of the things we struggle with have spiritual roots imbedded in spiritual laws we don't understand. And the only way to understand them is to seek out the ancient, religious texts that teach us about them.

While there are many texts from ancient cultures and religions, one in particular seems to be the most accurate. That text is the Bible. And as I've tested and applied its spiritual laws, I've seen people get freedom from all kinds of issues in their lives.

Because of that, as I walk you through the Prayer of Freedom I'll be using the ancient texts of the Bible as the primary source of these spiritual laws.

The second thing I want to talk about is how to *effectively pray to God.*

When we have problems in our lives that won't go away, most of us eventually resort to praying to God... and we do it whether we believe he exists or simply hope that he does. As the saying goes, "There are no atheists in a plane that's about to crash."

Most of us turn to prayer because we realize we can't fix our problems, but if there is a God who created everything, we assume *he* can. So, we start praying... but nothing happens.

That leads us to another question we must answer: "Does God answer all prayers?"

The Bible suggests God responds to prayers that align with his spiritual laws.

One of those spiritual laws it teaches is, **"The prayers of a righteous person are highly effective."**

If that line creates tension for you, stay with me—because "righteous" in Scripture doesn't mean perfect, and this isn't meant to condemn or shame you. It's meant to show you that God responds to something specific. And once you understand what that is, things can begin to change.

If you want to be set free from your problems, you must understand this law. And to better understand it, we need to ask a few more questions....

The first is: "*Why* are the prayers of a righteous person highly effective?"

The answer is so simple most people miss it. Their prayers are effective because... are you ready for this? ... God *answers* them!

If God answered your prayers, they would be effective. If he doesn't answer them, then they aren't.

But this brings us to a second question: "What does *highly effective* mean?"

Suppose two people pray to God: one consistently gets everything he prays for and the other doesn't. If that were the case, then you could say the first person's prayers are "highly effective." Does that make sense?

In other words, if your prayers are "highly effective," it simply means you consistently get what you ask for.

But that's not all we learn from this spiritual law. There's more that we must understand if we're going to apply it to our lives. And to discover what that is we must dig a little deeper...

Notice it says, "The prayers of a *righteous* person are highly effective." That implies that the prayers of an unrighteous person are *not* effective.

In other words, if you want God to answer your prayers so they will be effective, you must be "righteous" by God's standards (not just a 'good person' by human standards).

This isn't as difficult as it may seem. But to know what it means we must ask a third and final question...

"If God answers some people's prayers more than others, what makes God more *inclined* to answer their prayers?"

And to answer this question, we must look at a pattern we see across most ancient cultures...

How to approach God in a way that leads to answered prayer

In most ancient cultures, God is seen as a powerful God who must be appeased when you do something wrong. That appeasement is to remove his wrath, and it usually takes the form of an animal sacrifice.

Then, after appeasing him, you confess you were wrong and express sorrow for what you did. By offering contrition, you hope to win his favor.

Finally, assuming you won his favor, then you make your request—such as victory in battle or a good harvest—and hope that he answers it.

In simpler terms, people were trying to approach God in a way they believed he would respond to. It's much like when you've been trying to get the government to respond to a request and keep getting sent from office to office. But once you use the correct form and send it to the right place, your request is approved.

That's a pattern we see across many ancient cultures. It's also the pattern found in the Old Testament of the Bible texts. And what's fascinating is when I've helped others apply *this* pattern, their prayers have instantly become "highly effective." Now, when they ask God to set them free, he answers their prayer and does it!

With that as the background, I now want to introduce the process of the Prayer of Freedom.

Turn the page and I'll show you how it can bring freedom to your life.

Be blessed!

Beatty Carmichael

P.S. If you're a Christian and would like a deeper look at how this process aligns with Scripture, I've included a section titled "**For Christian Friends**" in the **Appendix** before continuing. You're welcome to read that now or return to it later if questions arise as you continue. Since *The Prayer of Freedom* addresses a complex theological topic, I've intentionally simplified some aspects to make it easier to understand. In that section, I provide a more detailed explanation of the methodologies used. If that applies to you, review it now and then return here. If not, you can safely skip it—you won't miss anything needed to complete the process.

Before you begin...

There are two things you should know before beginning.

First — This book has two sections. **Part 1** is "*The Battle.*" In it, you'll learn what's going on, why it happens, and how to be set free. **Part 2** is the "*Field Manual*" where you'll find the actual Prayer of Freedom guided exercises that bring peace and freedom to your life.

Part 1 will help you understand this unique approach to prayer and how to maintain lasting freedom. It gives insight into what's happening spiritually so you can avoid falling back into the same situations you're facing today.

However, statistics show that most people don't finish the books they begin—and the heart of this book is actually the prayer process in Part 2. So even though Part 1 matters, if you tend not to finish books and have issues you're ready to get rid of, feel free to jump straight to Part 2 and begin the Field Manual process. It works even if you don't yet understand why it works. Then, once you're done, you can come back and read Part 1.

Second — If you want to share what you're learning, it's easy. At the top of this page is the website address: **ThePrayerOfFreedom.com**. Simply direct others to that link where they can learn more and access the book and related resources.

You don't have to walk through this process alone. Many people find doing the Prayer of Freedom is easier and more effective when they go through it with others who can answer questions, offer encouragement, and pray with them along the way. That's why we created *The Prayer of Freedom Community* at **ThePrayerOfFreedom.com/Community**—a simple online gathering place where people from around the world support each other as they work through the process together. If you would like guidance, fellowship, or prayer support as you begin, please join us there. You can also participate in one of our free, online Group Studies (when available), where people walk through the process with a leader and have opportunity to ask questions while reading this book. Go to the link above or scan the QR code below.

Now, turn the page and let's begin your journey into freedom!

– Part 1 –

The Battle

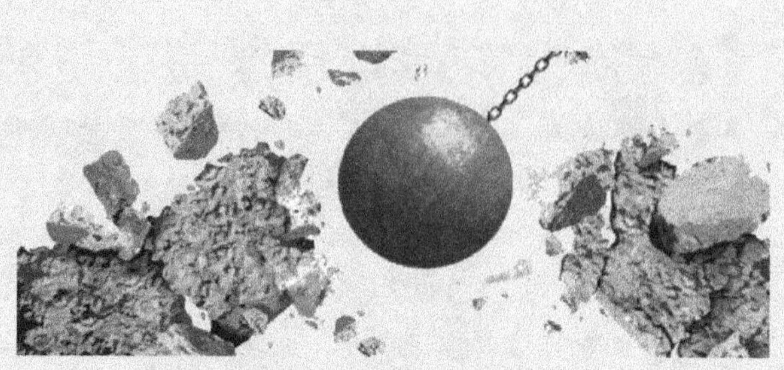

Start Here: A Quick Orientation

Watch a short video that shares a unique feature of this book to help you get best results.

Extra guidance is also provided for readers who have difficulty concentrating or reading for long periods.

Scan the QR code (or enter the URL) to watch now:

ThePrayerOfFreedom.com/Welcome

Author's Note: *If you haven't read the introduction yet, I want to invite you to begin*
Author's Note: *If you haven't read the introduction yet, I want to invite you to begin*
there. It gives a simple framework for why this book works and will help what follows make deeper sense.

— Chapter 1 —
Ancient spiritual laws of discipline and breakthrough

Penny grew up in a relatively normal home. As a religious person, she went to church every week and tried to live right to the best of her ability.

As we were talking one day, she shared that all through high school and college she had been healthy and never got sick. She was also quick to point out that she had remained a virgin until she started dating a certain guy in college. But three weeks before graduation, she gave herself to him and slept with him.

"What happened next was the beginning of a health nightmare," she said. "Within a few weeks, I got sick... and *stayed* sick for nearly twenty years!"

And just to be clear, this story isn't meant to shame anyone or claim every sickness has one simple cause. Here's what happened...

First, there was a car accident with a broken vertebra in her neck. Then, there was strep throat. Later, she was diagnosed with toxic shock. Then, she had strep throat a second time. Next, she was diagnosed with precancerous cells and underwent surgery to have them removed. She became an alcoholic and life continued spiraling downward. After that, she had several bronchial infections, strep throat for a third time... a fourth, fifth, sixth, and even seventh time!

At that point, she started living on antibiotics to try and combat all her sicknesses. During this time, she began suffering from constant joint and muscle pain, and the doctors finally diagnosed her as having chronic fatigue and fibromyalgia... with no cure.

That's when a friend explained the spiritual laws laid out in the Prayer of Freedom and guided her how to pray to God. Using those laws, Penny prayed to God and expressed sorrow for doing things he didn't want her doing ("repentance")—not just sleeping with her boyfriend, but other things she had done throughout the years. Then, she asked God to remove all her problems.

"That same day," she said, "*all* my sickness and addiction disappeared! No more fatigue, no more pain, no more stiffness in my limbs, no more strep throat, no more urge to drink—it was all gone!"

Now, fast forward to today...

"That was twenty years ago," Penny said, "and I am still free. *None* of the sicknesses have returned, and I haven't had another drink since!"

Her doctors claimed it was a "miracle." But it really wasn't. The source of her illnesses had been misdiagnosed for nearly twenty years. She simply did what God said to do—she repented. And when she did, he released her from the consequence of those things.

At this point, you may be wondering whether I'm saying her sickness was connected to sin. In Penny's case, yes—that's exactly what I'm saying. And while I don't know your story, I've seen similar patterns show up in many people's lives.

When you do wrong against God, the Bible calls it "sin." In other words, it's missing the mark of what God wants for you. And when you express sorrow for what you did and turn back toward him, the texts call it "repentance." These words aren't meant to shame or condemn—they simply describe how alignment with God works in real life.

Not all illness is connected to this, of course. But often, physical, emotional, and relational struggles trace back to places we drifted from God's design for us—not out of rebellion, but out of pain, confusion, or survival.

Regardless of how someone understands God—whether as a personal Creator, a Higher Power, or simply the ultimate Source—the point is this: there appears to be an objective spiritual order, and when we move out of alignment with it, the effects are real.

Some people use different language. In certain spiritual circles, harmful actions or ongoing patterns are often described as "low vibration" or "dark energy." The Bible uses the word *sin* to describe the same underlying condition. The language is different, but the idea is the same: when we move out of alignment with God, we create an opening for struggle in our lives.

So, if terms like "low vibration" or "dark energy" are more familiar to you, just know that when I use the word *sin* in this book, I'm referring to that same underlying reality. For simplicity, I'll use the biblical language from here forward.

And what I'm about to share with you—drawn from the ancient Bible texts—has the power to transform your life.

While you may not have all the issues Penny had, can you at least relate to what she went through? Maybe you have friends or loved ones experiencing something similar.

Would you believe me if I told you God may be using what you're facing—not to harm you, but to guide you toward real freedom?

Wait... what?! At this point, you're probably ready to stop reading and storm out of the room. Maybe you're thinking to yourself, "That doesn't make sense. How could God allow this? I thought God loves me and has a wonderful plan for my life. He wouldn't desire for me to suffer."

If that's you, I totally understand. But don't throw the book away just yet. Please hear me out. What I'm about to share might transform the way you think and change your life, just as it has changed mine and the lives of many others!

So, why would a loving God allow you—or my friend Penny—to suffer with so many issues?

It's because God *does* love you!

Let me explain...

God's plan is to give YOU abundant life

It's all part of a plan the God who created the universe put in place since the beginning of creation. And it has to do with his spiritual laws of discipline and our means of breakthrough.

As most of us travel through life we look at our earthly circumstances with earthly eyes, trying to figure out what we did that might be causing our problems. We try to make sense of what goes on around us... and most of the time we can't. So, we end up living a life full of struggles and frustration, with no way out.

But the good news is this: there really *is* a way out. You can be free from the darkness and heaviness in your life—free from chronic pain, depression, repeating failures, and other burdens that seem like they "just won't lift."

In the Bible, Jesus—whose teachings have influenced people around the world for centuries—said, "The thief comes to steal, kill, and destroy, but I came that you might have life, and have it abundantly" (**John 10:10**, paraphrased). Most people simply don't know how to step into that kind of life.

That's what you're about to learn—and it centers on a simple prayer process I call the Prayer of Freedom.

Discipline and conforming to the image of God's Son

A big part of what's going on is we only view life by what we see in the physical realm. But most of God's creation, and many of the things that directly impact our lives, are in the spiritual realm.

There are things going on in the spirit realm that we've never given any thought to. There are things God created and put in place to guide and train us. Yet, most of us have no awareness of them.

To show you what I mean, let's first look at another spiritual law found in the Bible. It comes from a book called Hebrews...

Hebrews 12:4-6—"In your struggle against sin [i.e. doing things God doesn't like]... do not make light of the Lord's discipline, and do not lose heart when he rebukes you. Because <u>the Lord disciplines the one he loves</u>, and he chastens everyone he accepts as his son." (ESV, clarification and emphasis added)

What does this say God does with those he "loves"?

He disciplines them!

If God loves you (which he does), he says he will discipline you. It's not that he *might* discipline you; he *will* discipline you. And just as a parent disciplines a child to correct and train him, it seems our heavenly Father does the same with us.

While on this topic, it's important to recognize that we are not being punished, we are being disciplined. *Discipline* and *punishment* are different. Discipline is for correction; punishment is for penalty. Discipline restores a person; punishment casts the person away. They feel similar because they both cause suffering. But it's the *purpose* of the suffering that differentiates the two.

God doesn't punish his children, but he *does* discipline them. What this means is, even if you are living what you consider a "righteous" life, God will still discipline you when you need to be corrected.

It's the same thing we do with our children. We set rules to guide and train them. If they break the rules, we discipline them. The purpose of the discipline isn't to *punish* them... it's to *correct* them so they learn to do things right.

That's what God does with us.

He sets the rules to guide and train us. When we break his rules, it's called "sin." As we've already seen, this doesn't mean you're bad; it means you missed the mark of what God wanted you to do in that moment—choosing something other than what was right.

And when we sin, God disciplines us to correct us, training us to do right, guiding us to conform into the image of his Son, Jesus (see **Romans 8:29**).

That's the key... conforming to the image of his Son. But what does that really mean?

Ancient Bible texts say that Jesus is God's Son. He is sinless and never did anything against God.

So, in a simplistic sense, to be "conformed to the image of his Son" means to sin *less* than we sin now and ultimately (though not humanly possible) become sinless—without sin, just as the Son is.

That's a main thing that sets us apart from the Son. We have sin, the Son does not. If we could become sinless, we would "be conformed to" his image.

Jesus modeled this life for us—fully God, yet fully Man—by living only as the Father directed (**John 5:19**). When we follow God's direction instead of our own desires, we begin to reflect His Son's image. But when we choose sin, we drift from that image, and that's where God's discipline comes in. Discipline is his loving way of correcting us, training us to turn from sin, and shaping us back into the image he originally intended for us. Anything outside that image is sin, and sin separates us from him.

Discipline originates in the spiritual realm, *even* for those who live "righteously"

What most people don't understand is God's discipline originates in the spiritual realm, but manifests in the earthly realm as issues in our lives.

How do I know? Because the ancient biblical texts teach it (as I'll show you in Chapters 7 and 8). I've also witnessed it firsthand—when people repent of past sins, their issues often disappear. This holds true not only for those leading "sinful" lives but also for those striving to live righteous lives.

For example, consider my friend Nick. A devoted follower of God and business owner for many years, he felt God calling him to leave his business and step into full-time ministry—and he faithfully obeyed.

That was about twenty years ago.

Today, he's an evangelist who has led hundreds of people to know God personally and is the pastor of a small church in his town.

He reached out to me one day because he had been in pain for several years and it had finally become unbearable. He had excruciating chest and back pain. It was so bad he couldn't even bend over or lift twenty pounds. The regular medical personnel couldn't figure out what the problem was, so he felt he needed to see a specialist.

I've learned that many things like this have a spiritual root—even from sins committed *many* years earlier—so I told Nick the first thing he ought to do was the Prayer of Freedom. So, following the same process I'll show you later, he made a list of sins he committed over the years, then repented of each one as he prayed through the Prayer of Freedom.

After *three days* he said, "**All of my pain is gone!** Both my chest and back pains are *completely* gone, and I can bend over again!" He couldn't believe it!

What this shows is we can't always look at our circumstances with "earthly glasses" to understand what's going on. Sometimes our issues may be due to spiritual laws of discipline rather than natural laws of cause-and-effect.

And if they are spiritual, you must put on "spiritual glasses" to understand the discipline and learn how to get free from it. That's what we're about to do in the next chapter.

But before we move into Chapter 2, I want to encourage you to take one simple step. If you're already sensing that your struggles may have a spiritual root and you're ready to begin breaking free, turn now to Part 2 and start by praying through the **Simplified Prayer**. It's the very first thing you'll find there.

This short prayer often brings remarkable breakthroughs, even before you go through the full Prayer of Freedom process. Once you've prayed through it, return here and continue to Chapter 2.

— Chapter 2 —
'Spiritual glasses' to see God's discipline

Dennis is an elderly man I've known for years. While visiting around the kitchen table one day, our conversation shifted to his adult son, Scott. For fifteen years, Scott and his family had been living in Dennis' house, unable to afford their own home.

Scott's career had started off strong in his mid-twenties, earning a multiple, six-figure income. But then, outside of his control, he was forced to change jobs and join a large corporation. A year later he was fired due to internal politics; and from that point forward Scott never recovered financially.

After years of trying to get back on his feet, he and his family eventually had to sell their home and move across the country to live with Scott's parents. During the next fifteen years he still couldn't "get ahead" financially. And even though he had faithfully followed God for over twenty-five years, something kept blocking him. He was consistently paid well below his skill level and he *still* couldn't afford to move out of his parents' home. These years were so difficult he began to feel like life had passed him by.

Back to the kitchen table...

As Dennis and I talked about these things, I suggested he pray the Prayer of Freedom on Scott's behalf. And as I mentioned earlier, all the prayer really is, is repenting of sins and asking God to remove any discipline tied to them.

Dennis wasn't sure how to do it, so I led him through it word for word, right there at the kitchen table. The sight was precious—an elderly father, lovingly praying on behalf of his adult son. The entire prayer lasted ten minutes. And then, cataclysmic shifts began happening in Scott's life.

Within three weeks Scott got an unexpectedly large pay raise at work, almost doubling his salary!

Three weeks after that, because of his increased income, he and his wife bought a new home. They could *finally* begin moving out of his parents' house.

Several months after that, Scott began getting all kinds of recognition at his job. So much so that he was asked to speak at national and international events to share what he was doing to consistently achieve such strong results.

Everything changed. It changed almost immediately. And what happened to change it was an elderly father praying the Prayer of Freedom on behalf of his adult son!

And yes—this isn't only for *you*. You can also use this process to help a loved one needing breakthrough.

I share this story because so many people live lives of "failure" and think, "That's just the way it is—I got dealt a bad hand." But depending on the root of the issues, there *can* be breakthrough from failure. All it takes is knowing where to look...

"Spiritual glasses" to look into the spiritual realm

In the last chapter, I explained how God's discipline comes from the spiritual realm. Now, let me take you on a short journey through the ways he disciplines us and what it might look like.

What I've come to realize over the years is the spiritual "warfare" most of us go through actually seems to play a large role in how God trains us. So, using that frame of reference, let's take a quick peek at what God tells us about spiritual warfare.

One early Bible text (**Ephesians 6:12**) puts it this way: "For we are not fighting against people made of flesh and blood, but against <u>persons without bodies</u>..." (TLB, emphasis added).

That's what our spiritual warfare is all about—it's fighting against *persons without bodies.*

Before going any further, I want to clarify something simple. A *spirit* is simply a "person" that exists in the spiritual realm rather than the physical one. That's where the word *spiritual* comes from, and why the Bible calls this *spiritual* warfare. It's not a fight against ideas or emotions—it's a conflict with real, non-physical spirits.

With that said, imagine I gave you a special pair of glasses that let you see into the spiritual realm. If you put them on in a room with other people, you would still see everyone you see now—but you would also become aware of other spirits present alongside them. They wouldn't have physical bodies though, because they exist in the spiritual realm rather than the earthly one.

This is the reality of the world we live in—we see people with physical bodies in the earthly realm, but there are also real spirits with us in the spiritual realm at the same time.

For example, one of the spirits you'd see is one you may have already heard about—the Holy Spirit. This is God's Spirit, and he is a real person. He simply doesn't have a physical body.

But that's not the only spirit you'd see. You'd also see angels. Angels are spirits who operate all around us in the spiritual realm. They are aware of what's going on, they have their own thinking, their own will, and their own personality. The only difference is not who they are, but where they exist. They have bodies in the spiritual realm, but not bodies of flesh and blood like we have in the earthly realm.

If you continue to look around with your spiritual glasses, you're likely to see other spirits as well. For example, just a few of the spirits the Bible mentions are a spirit of wisdom, a spirit of truth, a spirit of gentleness, and a spirit of skill.

Since all these spirits are 'good' spirits, we can refer to them *holy* spirits, because they tend to be present when people live in what the Bible calls holiness and righteousness.

However, as you continue looking around the room you might also see other spirits—spirits we could call *unholy* spirits. These are spirits the Bible mentions that tend to be present when people live unholy and unrighteous lives.

For example, you might see a spirit of fear around someone, maybe a spirit of lying or anger around another, and possibly even a spirit of jealousy around someone else. These are spirits connected to emotions, and in this case, *unholy* emotions.

Other unholy spirits you might see would be spirits of infirmity. Infirmity is anything you might go to the doctor for (i.e. mental health, chronic pain, and persistent illnesses). The bottom line is, if you suffer with mental or physical issues that would not be considered perfect health, there may be a spirit of infirmity involved.

In fact, the Bible mentions quite a few spirits of infirmity; among them are a spirit of fever, deafness, muteness, blindness, lameness, crooked spine, and even a spirit of seizures.

These all fall into the category of infirmities, and many times they may be caused by spirits—by "persons without bodies" in the spiritual realm. I know it sounds a little spooky, but it's true. And it's all in the Bible. Let me show you one example.

At one point, Jesus is teaching in a synagogue when a woman comes in who had been hunched over, unable to straighten up, for eighteen years. It was a spirit of infirmity. How do we know? Because the Bible text tells us. Let's read it now...

Luke 13:10-13—"On a Sabbath Jesus was teaching in one of the synagogues, and a woman was there who had been crippled by a spirit for eighteen years. She was bent over and could not straighten up at all. When Jesus saw her, he called her forward and said to her, 'Woman, you are set free from your infirmity.' Then he put his hands on her, and immediately she straightened up and praised God." (NIV, emphasis added)

When Luke says she was "crippled by a spirit," that means it was a spirit of infirmity that had been tormenting (crippling) the woman for eighteen years. And how did she get healed? Jesus declared she was set free, and the spirit left.

Here's the interesting thing, though. Nothing you're about to learn falls outside God's order and care.

As I introduce the next idea, parts of it may seem unfamiliar or even hard to accept at first. That's okay. You don't have to agree with the framework I'm about to share for the process to work. For now, simply stay with the idea and notice what happens as you read and apply it.

"Spirits of Discipline"

Regardless of the specific actions each spirit may carry out, it seems that part of their role is connected to the way discipline shows up in our lives. I call them "spirits of discipline" because this appears to be a key function they serve in the process God uses to bring discipline and correction into our lives when we sin.

In other words, spirits of discipline seem to be one of the ways God helps train us in righteousness. The purpose of discipline is to bring us to repentance and, ultimately, conform us into *his* image (the image of his Son). Everything He allows or guides us through in life is directed toward that purpose.

How do you become conformed to God's image? By turning away from the sinful things that block His image in us.

It's like a child who gets disciplined because he disobeyed his father. After being disciplined for the same issue again and again, he eventually learns to stop doing it and he no longer gets disciplined for it.

Within this framework, it's as if God uses spirits of discipline to bring us back to repentance when we sin. And when we repent and stop doing those things, the discipline seems to no longer be needed.

But here's the key—even though we may be living righteously *today*, spirits of discipline could be causing problems in our lives from sin we committed years ago. In other words, simply because we've stopped those sins and have lived righteously ever since doesn't mean the discipline for them has stopped. And this is what I consistently see—it seems the discipline only stops when we *repent* of those sins.

That means if you suffer with chronic pain, sickness or mental health, then even if you've been living righteously for years, those problems *could* be tied to sins from years back… and often from early childhood.

Spirits of discipline and tow truck drivers

When I was teaching on this topic before, one lady expressed her concern, "Help me understand how a loving God would send a spirit of discipline to bring all kinds of sickness or misery to someone? That just doesn't seem like the God I know and love."

In case you're thinking the same thing, let me clarify what's going on. God is *not* sending a spirit of discipline upon anyone. However, the spiritual laws he created allow for it to happen *automatically*.

Here's an easy way to understand it…

Imagine a popular restaurant in a university town, right across from the campus and surrounded by dormitories. If you're familiar with university towns, you know parking is always in short supply. With such a prime location, it's tempting for students to park there while they head to class or visit friends in the dorms. However, the restaurant owner doesn't want this—it would take up valuable space for customers and hurt his business.

So, how does he solve this problem?

First, he makes an agreement with a towing company that gives them the legal right to tow any car in his parking lot that is not a customer. Then, he posts signs that read, *"For restaurant customers only! All unauthorized vehicles will be towed!"* You've seen those signs before, right?

What happens next is this...

The towing company sends out trucks driven by employees whose sole job is to look for illegally parked cars. They get paid for every car they find and tow, so they are motivated to look everywhere, all the time, to find the next violator. And as soon as they find one, they have a legal right to tow the car and charge the student a lot of money to get his car back.

Now that you've got the scenario, here's one way it could play out in real life...

Jim needs to give some papers to a friend who's studying on campus. It's late at night, the restaurant is closed, the parking lot is empty, and the building where his friend is studying is just a few minutes' walk from the restaurant parking lot. So, Jim swings into the parking lot, walks across the street to drop off the papers, and returns. The entire process takes less than fifteen minutes—but by the time he gets back, his car is gone. The tow truck already came and took it away!

Jim is obviously upset. After all, he was only there fifteen minutes. Not only that, but the parking lot was *empty*—the restaurant wasn't even using it at that moment, so it wasn't hurting anyone to park there. The towing company took his car and is now asking for a lot of money to get it back. It doesn't seem fair.

So, who can Jim complain to?

It wasn't the restaurant owner's fault. In fact, the owner never *sent* the tow truck to take Jim's car away. So, Jim can't complain to the owner.

It wasn't the towing company's fault. The towing company had a legal right to remove any violator who parked there illegally, regardless of what time it was. So, he can't complain to them.

It was Jim's fault! He saw the signs and he knew the risks involved. But he thought it wasn't a big deal—he thought he could "get away with it."

In a sense, that is how the process works with us and spirits of discipline. It's a legal structure with rules set up by God, and the whole thing operates automatically. The rules and consequences are posted in the Bible. God doesn't *send* spirits of discipline against us, but they are constantly present and actively looking for violations. As soon as we break the rules, they have legal access to bring discipline into our lives.

Before continuing, one clarification will help you read what follows correctly.

Identifying a spiritual cause is not the same as assigning personal blame. Many forms of suffering involve access in the spiritual realm without fault, intent, or awareness on your part. These explanations are meant to give context, not to judge.

So, how do spirits of discipline work?

That's what we'll cover in the next chapter.

— Chapter 3 — How spirits of discipline work

Thirteen-year-old Riley asked, "Is it normal to feel physically *lighter* after doing this?" as she giddily danced around the kitchen.

I had known Riley and her family for over ten years, and in the past six years I had never seen Riley smile, let alone *dance* for joy. Now, she was skipping about the house, humming to herself, and had the biggest smile you could imagine!

Beaming from ear to ear at what God had just done in her life, I answered, "Yes, it is. That's what freedom feels like."

Fifteen minutes earlier, she was a different person. So different that you wouldn't even believe this was the same girl. For the last number of years, she had always been depressed and sullen. She was dark—in her appearance, the way she dressed, her personality, her outlook on life. But something changed when I led her through the simple Prayer of Freedom.

I was at her home because, a few days earlier, her mom served divorce papers against her dad. Her life was crumbling around her, and I was there to help the family pray through these issues.

When I first spoke with her that day, I asked, "Riley, do you ever feel like you're carrying a heavy load around all the time, like a great, big backpack filled with rocks?"

From her hunched over position, I could barely make out her mumbled reply, "Yes. It feels like a *heavy* backpack."

I went on to ask, "Do you feel darkness in your life?"

"All the time!" came her immediate response as she looked up at me. I had obviously struck a nerve.

"Do you feel depressed?" "Yes," she said.

That's when I guided her through the Prayer of Freedom. And after she prayed, *all* of it disappeared immediately! All the darkness, all the heaviness weighing her down, depression... everything.

Now, you may not be a thirteen-year-old girl, but I bet you can relate to what Riley was going through.

If Riley's story resonates with you, it's because the same underlying dynamics often show up in adult lives as well—just in different forms.

What Riley experienced wasn't hype or emotion—it was a real shift she could feel immediately. And before we go further, it's important to know this: you don't have to understand everything for the Prayer of Freedom to work. But if you do understand what's happening beneath the surface, it can help you stay hopeful and confident as

God begins lifting the weight.

God and Michelangelo—how God conforms us to his image

An easy way to understand how God conforms us to his image is to think of a sculptor carving a beautiful marble statue.

One of the most famous statues in the world is *David* by Michelangelo. When people asked how he created such a masterpiece from a single block of stone, Michelangelo reportedly said, "I saw the person inside the stone—and carved away everything that wasn't part of him until I set him free."

Michelangelo was a master sculptor and worked with great intention. He used different tools—first to remove what clearly didn't belong, then to refine what remained, until the person was fully revealed.

In a similar way, God works with us.

The focus of discipline is to chip away what does not conform to his image.

In the beginning, when God created humanity, we were made in his image. But when sin entered the picture, that image was lost. Over time, sin clung to humanity, forming a block of "stone" around us. By the time we were born, we were already encased in a "block of sin"—still God's children, but no longer reflecting his image.

Just as Michelangelo used tools to remove everything that didn't belong to the person within the stone, God's process works in a similar way. Spirits of discipline function as tools—applying pressure that brings us to repentance. And it is repentance that removes the sin and allows God's image to come through.

As that happens, God's image becomes increasingly clear in us.

This is a framework—not a picture of God wielding spirits against us, but of how his spiritual laws naturally respond when sin opens a door and repentance closes it.

Spirits of discipline and repentance

As I mentioned before, when you break the rules, it's called "sin." And when you acknowledge you were wrong and turn the other direction, it's called "repentance." That's the goal of discipline: to bring about repentance.

When we sin against God, it's the spirits of discipline that seem to help guide us to repentance so we can be conformed back to God's image. This appears to be how God's process works.

We first see this in the Bible through a man named John the Baptist. His central message was simple: "Repent!" And when Jesus began his ministry, he preached the same message: "Repent! For the kingdom of heaven is in your midst." Everything else he taught flows out of that call.

Repentance is the key to conforming back to the image of God!

(If you're a Christian and the phrase "spirits of discipline" raises questions, don't get stuck here. This will make more sense as we continue. A more complete biblical framing is available in the Appendix under ***For Christian Friends****, sub-section "Simplicity Over Precision.")*

The two consequences of sin

Before we go further, here's a brief framework that helps explain why repentance matters so much.

In very simple terms, sin does two things.

First, sin breaks our relationship with God.

Man was created to have fellowship with God. And as long as Man (represented by the first man, Adam) remained without sin, that relationship was intact. However, as soon as Adam sinned, the relationship was broken... and it's been broken ever since.

Second, sin breaks our image of God.

Man was created in the image of God. That image was a perfect, righteous, sinless image. But when Adam sinned, it broke his image of God, and all future generations have been made in *Adam's* image, not God's image (**Genesis 5:3**). Our image of God has been broken ever since.

So, how do we restore our *relationship* with God?

We repent of our sins *as a whole* and believe in Jesus's death to have freed us from those sins. By faith, believing in Jesus and repenting of our sins, our relationship is restored with Father God.

But what about God's image—how do we restore the *image* of God?

It's similar, but slightly different. We repent of our sins, but instead of repenting of them as a whole, we repent of them individually as God brings them to mind—one at a time, not by hunting every failure down, but by letting Him surface what needs to be cleared.

Since each individual sin breaks a portion of God's image from us, we must repent of each sin individually for that portion of His image to be restored. This is how God's discipline works—it tends to remain in a specific area until the specific sin is repented of.

If this feels different from what you've been taught, stay with me. I'll walk you through the Scriptural foundation for it step by step over the next several chapters.

This process works for anyone, regardless of religious background. I've consistently seen pain, depression, and other problems disappear when specific sins are addressed.

Here's a text message from a friend that illustrates this. I had spoken with her husband the day before and guided him through a simplified version of the Prayer of

Freedom. His wife then shared what happened...

"Good morning! I cannot thank you enough for taking time to walk Kyle through the freedom prayer yesterday. In spite of chiropractic therapy, his spine has been twisting and his shoulders have become visibly lopsided over the past year or two. He has literally been shrinking before our eyes. When he came home last night, he was **over 2 inches taller** and restored to his normal height! Spine straight, back pain almost completely gone, shoulders even. Unburdened. THANK YOU!"

You don't need to remember or identify everything yourself—God will bring to mind what needs to be addressed, at the right time.

Now that we have a glimpse of the process and what spirits of discipline are for, let's look at some of the methods they may use in our lives. To do that, we'll need to go back in time to the Middle Ages...

— Chapter 4 —
Parable of the Unmerciful Servant

Medieval England, Circa 1450 A.D.

The dungeon was quiet now.

"Not peaceful—just quiet in the way places become when everyone already knows what happens there. Prisoners sat along the stone walls, speaking in murmurs, listening for footsteps they never wanted to hear.

Deep below, there was a room no one entered willingly.

That was where *the device* was kept.

It wasn't kept there because the king delighted in suffering. It was kept there because the kingdom had laws—and when someone broke them, consequences followed. The device existed for one purpose: to apply pressure that remained until a person finally responded.

Some called it the rack.

Unsettling, yes. But the point isn't the device itself. The point is this: when pressure is applied long enough, it eventually produces a response.

And that's where this becomes relevant.

Jesus tells a parable that reveals something sobering about God's kingdom: certain sins can place a person under a form of discipline that does not lift until repentance closes the door.

Let me explain...

The Parable of the Unmerciful Servant

In another story about Jesus, he shares a parable called the Parable of the Unmerciful Servant. Let's look at it.

Matthew 18:21 (NIV)—"Then Peter came to Jesus and asked, 'Lord, how many times shall I forgive my brother or sister who sins against me? Up to seven times?'"

I want to set up this scenario for you here. As he usually does, Peter thinks he's going above and beyond what he should be doing here—"As many as *seven* times?! This is great. That's gotta be a lot, right?"

But Jesus, as he does so many times (with all of us), lovingly corrects Peter. Here's what he says:

v. 22—"Jesus answered, 'I tell you, not seven times, but seventy times seven.'"

Next, Jesus tells a story, called a parable, to articulate a spiritual truth about God's kingdom.

vv. 23-24—"Therefore, the kingdom of heaven is like a king who wanted to settle accounts with his servants. As he began the settlement, a man who owed him ten thousand bags of gold was brought to him..."

Just to put that into perspective, that's many *billions* USD today!

vv. 25-26—"Since he was not able to pay, the master ordered that he and his wife and his children and all that he had be sold to repay the debt. At this, the servant fell on his knees before him, 'Be patient with me,' he begged, 'And I will pay back everything.'"

Do you think he could?

No way. It's too much.

vv. 27-28a—"The servant's master took pity on him, cancelled the debt, and let him go. But when that servant went out, he found one of his fellow servants who owed him one hundred silver coins..."

One hundred silver coins is about $10,000 USD in today's terms. This shows the magnitude of difference between the two servants' debts.

vv. 28b-34—"He grabbed him and began to choke him, 'Pay back what you owe me!' he demanded. His fellow servant fell to his knees and begged him, 'Be patient with me, and I will pay it back.' But he refused. Instead, he went off and had the man thrown into prison until he could pay the debt. When the other servants saw what had happened, they were outraged and went and told their master everything that had happened. Then, the master called the servant in, 'You wicked servant!' he said, 'I cancelled all that debt of yours because you begged me to. Shouldn't you have had mercy on your fellow servant just as I had on you?' In anger, his master handed him over to the jailers to be tortured until he should pay back all that he owed."

Now, if you look at various Bible translations of this passage, you'll find that some versions only use the word 'jailer' and leave out the 'tortured' part of it. But when that happens, you'll usually find a footnote that says, "Some manuscripts also include 'to be tortured.'"

Jesus is telling a story about something important here. But what does it have to do with Peter's question regarding forgiveness? And what in the world does it have to do with spirits of discipline?

Let me see if I can paint this picture for you so we can go a little deeper...

This parable is about a country ruled by a king with subjects who live in it. The king sets rules on how his kingdom should operate. If you break the rules, you are disciplined.

So, what's the role of the jailer in all of this?

It's discipline—if you break the rules, you visit the jailer and he performs the discipline.

The Greek word being translated as 'jailer' means: "a torturer; a person who extracts the truth from others through use of the rack." And the rack was a tool used to torture someone.

That's why a person was sent to the jailer—to face the consequences of wrongdoing.

So, think about this...

It's not likely the king and the jailer are friends. It's not likely they are in the same socio-economic circles of kingdom society.

While you have an evil, ugly jailer in the dungeon, at the same time you have the king in his castle. He's clean, majestic, wearing royal robes, and he loves his subjects. The two are so diametrically opposed that they don't even seem to go together.

Yet, the jailer plays a significant role in the kingdom, and the king allows him to be there.

No one *wants* to see the jailer, so they do good. But if they do bad, they are sent to the jailer. And when they come back out again, they don't want to do bad anymore. That makes sense, right?

With that, now we get to the main message Jesus is teaching in his parable.

Keep in mind, Jesus is not telling this parable to the Jewish leaders. He's not talking to the Pharisees, or to the people who have rejected him. He's not even talking to the crowds who come and listen to him. Jesus is talking to his closest disciples. He's talking to Peter and the twelve apostles. And here's what he says...

v. 35 - "This is how my Heavenly Father will treat each of you, unless you forgive your brother from your heart."

Notice he doesn't say, "My Heavenly Father *might* do this." He says, "My Heavenly Father *will* do this."

What Jesus is talking about is *discipline*—in this case, for unforgiveness. Unforgiveness is a sin. And because all sins are similar—they all break the image of God—they all have a similar process of correction.

That correction is discipline. But discipline comes in different forms. Just as with children— sometimes a child receives immediate correction, at other times they are given a time-out, and other times they lose privileges. Regardless of the form, it's all discipline to bring about correction.

It's the same with God. His discipline may take different forms for each person and for each sin, but it's all discipline, nonetheless. That's what Jesus is conveying to us.

Notice, too, that in this parable the king doesn't *send* the jailer against anyone. The only way someone ends up with the jailer is through their own wrongdoing. In other words, it's their actions, not the king's, that result in their discipline.

Similarly, God doesn't send spirits of discipline upon us, either. In the parable, the king represents God, the servants represent us, and the jailer represents a spirit of discipline. We saw how it works in the parable; now, let's look at how it works in the

Bible:

When we have unrepented sin, Satan—referred to as "the accuser of the brethren" **(Revelation 12:10)**—acts as a prosecutor in God's heavenly "courtroom." He accuses us of sins before the Judge, who is God. If we are found guilty, we receive a judgment of discipline—and it is enforced in the spiritual realm until we repent.

So, as you can see, it's not *God* who sends these spirits against us. We bring it upon *ourselves* when we sin and allow ourselves to be accused by Satan.

And that brings us to another question: *how* does God, our Heavenly Father, discipline us?

Well, a little sleuthing around in the world of Greek translations will reveal a startling truth.

When you look at the word translated as "jailer," the root of that word comes from a Greek word called *basanizo*. And it's this *basanizo* that is the form through which much of God's discipline comes to us.

Let's look at it now—it will surprise you.

Keep going even if this feels unfamiliar. You don't need perfect understanding for this to work.

— Chapter 5 — Three forms of "*basanizo*" discipline

My wife and I are friends with a single mom named Jan. She has two young children and has recently been going through nasty legal problems with her ex-husband.

He had been criminally accused of things related to why the divorce happened, and whenever he spends time with the kids the court requires him to be supervised for the children's safety. Even so, every time the kids are with him, they're terrified. Just the mention that they are going to spend time with their father scares them.

Despite the charges against him, the ex-husband was still trying to gain custody of the kids and do all he could to reduce his child support.

For months, neither of the children would talk about their fear, and whenever Jan asked, they would just close up. But she kept praying that their "voices" would be heard so the court could better understand the situation and protect them.

When harm comes upon a person from another, it isn't sin on their part. Being harmed does not make them guilty. At the same time, when someone else causes that harm, it can open spiritual access to the one being harmed—and that access can be removed without assigning blame to them.

When Jan shared this, I just felt in my heart that it was a spiritual battle more than anything else. That's when I suggested Jan pray the Prayer of Freedom.

And she did.

About two or three days later she told me, "I prayed that prayer you sent me and there were *significant* breakthroughs with the children. Both of them, individually, started opening up to me on their own about their dad. They started talking and sharing their feelings about how he scares them. And it wasn't just a short conversation either—it was a *flood* of conversation. Each one just kept talking and talking as if their voices had been dammed up for a long time and the dam finally burst, letting it all come out!"

It was such a breakthrough for Jan that she was almost in tears.

If you've never been in a similar situation, it may not seem like a big deal to you. But for Jan, who was at her wits end on how to get the children to open up so the judge could hear their side of the story, it was *huge*!

And it was, in some mysterious way, a spirit of discipline that was holding them back.

Spirits of discipline operate in various ways. For Jan, they were blocking the children's voices from being heard. For others, it's something else.

Let's look now at three of the most common ways these spirits operate...

Basanizo discipline

As I mentioned in the last chapter, the root word in the Greek for 'jailer' is *basanizo*. This word means: "to torture, to inflict pain, to torment."

As you'll see in Scripture, *basanizo* is the process through which discipline occurs. This word is used only twelve times in the New Testament, and we'll look at three passages that show how this kind of discipline appears in real life.

I believe it will help because once you recognize it, you will no longer look with earthly eyes at your earthly circumstances and say, "These issues I'm going through are simply due to natural causes," or "I have no idea why I'm going through these things." Instead, once you understand what you're looking for, you can say, "This feels like a spirit of discipline in my life Let me think through what I might have done that would have opened the door to be disciplined." Then, with the Prayer of Freedom, you'll be able to stop it.

Let's look now at what basanizo does in our lives...

▸ *Basanizo* Discipline #1 - physical suffering

The first passage is found in Matthew 8 with the story of a centurion and his sick servant.

Matthew 8:5-6—"When he had entered Capernaum, a centurion came forward to him, appealing to him, 'Lord, my servant is lying paralyzed at home, <u>suffering</u> terribly.'" (ESV)

"Suffering" is the word *basanizo*. Here, it shows up as paralysis—**physical suffering.**

Physical suffering is one form of *basanizo* discipline—it can manifest in any part of your body as something that isn't functioning properly.

I remember one day when my wife and I were at Walmart. We saw a young, homeless couple named Nita and Brad outside the entrance, so we asked if we could pray for them. In the conversation they mentioned they had just been given an apartment, so we took them inside to buy a few things to help them set up their new home.

While we were there, I picked up a book on spiritual growth for them. And as we were walking down the aisle, I was teasing Brad, saying, "You'll have to fight Nita for the book if you want to read it."

But Nita said, "Oh no, Brad will read it to me because I can't read."

I went, "Aww, I'm sorry. I didn't know you couldn't read. What happened... have you never learned?"

And she said, "Oh, no, it's not that. I know how to read, but I just can't see to read. Everything is blurry."

At that point, Nita was standing several feet from Brad. This was during wintertime and Brad had on a knit ski cap with large, two-inch tall letters on it that read, "LEVI'S." I asked, "Can you read the word on his hat?"

She said, "No, the letters are too blurry."

So I said, "Well, I don't think God wants you to have blurry vision. Let's pray for it."

I then led her through a short version of the Prayer of Freedom. And in asking her questions about things that might be unrepented sins, I asked if she had unforgiveness in her heart for anyone.

She admitted, "Yes, my ex-boyfriend. He grabbed me by the hair on the back of my head and slammed my face into the dresser over and over again, breaking out all my teeth, top and bottom." To verify, she showed me she had no teeth in the front of her mouth.

I asked if she would be willing to forgive him, and she said yes. So I led her in a short prayer of forgiveness. Then, I asked God to open her eyes so she could see clearly.

To test it out, I asked her again if she could read the word "LEVI'S" on Brad's hat, and this time, she could! I then opened the book we got for them, held it about four feet away, and asked if she could read it, too.

... And she DID! She began reading the book from four feet away. God perfectly restored her vision!

It seems her blurry eyesight was due to a spirit of discipline—a physical suffering impacting her eyes that left when she repented.

That's one form of *basanizo*.

▸ *Basanizo* Discipline #2 - mental suffering

The second passage we'll look at is in 2 Peter where it is talking about sin, fallen angels, and the like. We'll pick up the passage here...

2 Peter 2:7-8—"And if he rescued righteous Lot, greatly distressed by the sensual conduct of the wicked (for as that righteous man lived among them day after day, he was <u>tormenting</u> his righteous soul over their lawless deeds that he saw and heard)." (ESV)

"Tormenting" is the Greek word *basanizo*. And in this case, it's used to describe **mental suffering.**

How does this play out with us today?

I remember a story from a pastor named Richard. His son, Andy, was a youth pastor. Andy went through a nasty divorce that his wife initiated. It was terrible. It tore Andy up and he went spiraling downward. He became so depressed that he lost his job and couldn't even leave the house for *two* years.

His pastor-dad was on his knees every day battling for his son in prayer, but nothing ever changed.

Then, one day God opened Richard's eyes to understand more about the foundational truths behind the Prayer of Freedom. God told Richard to repent on behalf of his son. So Richard repented for all the sins he imagined Andy had probably been dealing with—anger, frustration, hurt, unforgiveness, all these things. The entire prayer session lasted about fifteen minutes. That's it.

About ten days later, Andy calls up Richard and says, "Dad, you won't believe what happened. Ten days ago, the depression instantly left! I am totally normal now!"

It was a spirit of discipline—mental suffering in the form of depression—and it lasted until those sins were repented of. An interesting thing about this case, too, is it was his *father* who repented for his sins, not himself (like what happened with the elderly father in Chapter 2 who repented on *his* son's behalf).

▸ *Basanizo* Discipline #3 - physical pain

The third example I want to share is from the last book in the Bible, called Revelation. It shows yet another form *basanizo* can take in our lives.

Revelation 12:2—"She was pregnant and was crying out in birth pains and the agony of giving birth." (ESV)

"Agony" is the Greek word *basanizo*. And in this instance, *basanizo* shows up as **physical pain**.

Another experience I had with *basanizo* discipline was at the drug addiction recovery center where I teach as a volunteer. Word had spread about my praying for people, and a woman named Susan came up and asked if I would pray for her.

I said "Sure, what's wrong?"

She said, "I've had rheumatoid arthritis for fifteen or twenty years, and it's *really* been flaring up these last several days."

So, I began going through the Prayer of Freedom with her; and as I did, I asked, "Do you have unforgiveness for anyone?"

She said, "Yes."

"Would you be willing to forgive them?"

Again, she said, "Yes."

I led her in a condensed version of the Prayer of Freedom, "Lord, I forgive so and so..." After that, I asked God to take away her arthritis pain. Then, I asked her to test it out.

She went up and down a flight of stairs, and when she came back, she exclaimed, "It feels a *lot* better!"

After I left, I didn't give it much thought until a few weeks later. I had just finished teaching a class when Susan walked in. She tracked me down because she wanted to give me an update. And this is what she said...

"Ever since we prayed that prayer five weeks ago, I've had *no* arthritis pain."

I said, "Praise God! That's wonderful!"

She continued, "I just came back from the doctor last week. He retested me and told me that I don't have *any* arthritis in my body at all."

Again, I said, "That's wonderful!"

But then, she said one more thing that was even more amazing....

She went on, "... not only that, but the doctor said my body shows no signs of *ever* having had arthritis in the past!"

It was simply a spirit of discipline in the form of physical suffering.

This is one of the things I often see. When a sickness is due to a spirit of discipline and you repent of the sin for which you're being disciplined, not only does the discipline stop but, frequently, God will restore the *physical* damage that the discipline created!

It's mind-boggling and exciting, don't you think?

But what does all of this mean?

What it means to me is simple...

When you go through any kind of challenge in your life—aches, pains, relationship conflicts, and more—it might be a spirit of discipline. And if it is, all it takes to stop the suffering is the Prayer of Freedom in Chapter 12!

One more concept to make sense of suffering tied to sin and discipline is "legal rights"—and understanding it will make a big impact when it comes to freedom.

— Chapter 6 —
Legal Rights

Before explaining legal rights, let me show you how they work.

A friend of mine, Bill, is in his early 50's. About thirty-five years ago he broke his right hip playing college football and has been in pain ever since. The pain had been getting progressively worse over the years. Anytime he walked, the pain was excruciating! By the time I spoke with him a few months ago (as of the time I'm writing this), it had become so severe that he had been walking with a cane for over a year.

In fact, it was so bad that the doctors had been telling him for the last several years he needed full hip replacement surgery.

What Bill was experiencing didn't appear to be random or fully explained by natural causes. So, I stepped in to help him find out what it was…

As he was sharing about his hip, my heart felt like this was probably a *basanizo*-type discipline rather than just natural causes, so I began asking a few questions. Going through the Prayer of Freedom process, I was looking for any unrepented sins he might have done before his accident that could be at its root.

As we talked, he shared that he was sexually active in high school. Since I couldn't find any other significant sin he had done, I felt that may have been the issue we were looking for. So, I led him in a short version of the Prayer of Freedom, had him repent of that sin, then asked God to heal his hip.

What happened next was amazing!

I asked him to stand up and check it out.

He stood up and started crying. Now, Bill is a big guy, so I wasn't expecting that at all!

After about two or three minutes, he regained his composure and said, "Beatty, I'm *completely* out of pain!" He started walking around the house without his cane, and without *any* pain.

This was the first time in thirty-five years that his hip was pain-free—the pain was completely gone! God gave him a new hip, healing the physical damage caused by the discipline (just as he did for Susan in the previous chapter, who had struggled with arthritis for years).

Over time, I've learned that when an injury doesn't heal and only grows worse, it's often a sign of basanizo discipline at work.

The pain was a physical issue in which all the x-rays and tests showed the hip was worn out and needed to be fully replaced. The doctors had confirmed it multiple times. But even though there was physical damage, the ultimate root behind it was spiritual.

The spiritual root was unrepented sin.

This is what the Parable of the Unmerciful Servant shows us. If you sin and disobey God, and don't repent of that sin, then God will allow a spirit of discipline in your life *for your own good.* He wants to bring correction in your life and guide you to repentance. He doesn't do this to punish you, but to bring you back into alignment, helping conform you into the image of his Son.

And as I mentioned back in the first chapter, God does this because he loves you.

God's discipline is for our good... *because* he loves us

Now, let's look at a few more passages from the Bible that show God's ultimate purpose with all of this. The first one is from Hebrews.

Hebrews 12:7b-11—"For what children are not disciplined by their fathers? ... We have all had human fathers who disciplined us, and we respected them for it... They disciplined us for a little while as they thought best. But <u>God disciplines us for our good</u>, in order that we may share in his holiness. No discipline seems pleasant at the time, but painful. Later on, however, it produces a harvest of <u>righteousness and peace</u> for those who have been trained by it." (NIV, emphasis added)

Notice two things about God's discipline. First, it's "for our good." And second, it brings forth "righteousness and peace" in our lives.

While discipline produces righteousness and peace, a lack of peace often points to unresolved sin.

If your life is filled with constant frustration and turmoil—either with relationship problems, external problems beyond your control, job issues, chronic health problems, anger, infertility, and the like—and you have no peace in those areas, the root problem may simply be unrepented sin.

To illustrate this even more, let's look at a passage in the Gospel of John. This is about a lame man at the pool. Now that you're learning more about *basanizo* discipline, if you are familiar with this passage, it might make more sense to you now as to what's really going on. We find it in **John 5:2-9, 14** (ESV)...

vv. 2-3—"Now there is in Jerusalem by the Sheep Gate a pool, in Aramaic called Bethesda, which has five roofed colonnades. In these lay a multitude of invalids—blind, lame, paralyzed."

The spirit of basanizo shows up here as physical suffering—"blind, lame, paralyzed."

vv. 5-9, 14a—"One man was there who had been an invalid for thirty-eight years. When Jesus saw him lying there and knew that he had already been there a long time... Jesus said to him, 'Get up, take up your bed, and walk.' And at once the man was healed, and he took up his bed and walked... Afterward, Jesus found him in the temple and said to him, 'See, you are well...'"

Now watch this. For anyone familiar with this passage, this is the part most don't understand...

v. 14b—"Sin no more, that nothing *worse* may happen to you." (emphasis added)

It appears there was a spirit of discipline bringing *basanizo* torment in the form of paralysis and physical suffering. We infer from Jesus' final statement that this man must have done something in the past to bring this discipline on himself. Otherwise, why would Jesus tell him, "Sin no more, that nothing *worse* may happen to you?" He didn't say that to everyone he healed, but he *did* say it to this man!

From this passage, it seems God may allow spirits of discipline to bring suffering—not as punishment, but as correction. That pain becomes a teacher, leading us to repentance and shaping us more closely into the image of God.

The process *always* begins with repentance. You repent first, then you get breakthrough. You repent first, then you get freedom.

Why? Because repentance is turning away from the sin that holds us back from conforming to him. It's the chipping away of the "stone" of sin that blocks our image of God.

Unrepented sin and "legal rights"

Unrepented sin gives spirits of discipline a "legal right" to torment us. This is the key to understanding God's discipline and how the Prayer of Freedom works.

Remember, spirits of discipline are usually *unholy* spirits. Unholy spirits are those that oppose God. They don't like God. Yet, in some mysterious way, they are all part of God's creation. Even if he didn't create them that way, they are one of his methods to bring us to repentance.

If you go back to the jailer in the Parable of the Unmerciful Servant, this process starts to make more sense...

The jailer hates the king and doesn't like serving him. But when people break the law, they go before a judge who renders a judgment and sends them to the dungeon. The judgment notice goes with the accused and is given to the jailer.

That judgment says you have been convicted of breaking the law, and it's that conviction that serves as the legal right for the jailer to do what he loves to do: to cause pain in your life.

In the spirit world, the legal right is unrepented sin. It gives these spirits of discipline a right to torment us, and when someone has unrepented sin giving them a legal right to attack, those spirits are *unable* to resist—they are wired to respond. And bringing pain, torment, and suffering is the only thing they know how to do, and they *long* to do it.

If this feels like a lot to process, stay with me. As we go on, I'll continue to show the Scriptural foundation for this, and it will become clearer step by step.

The thief that destroys

Jesus speaks about these spirits in **John 10:10**—"The thief comes only to steal, kill and destroy. I came that [you] may have life and have it abundantly." (ESV, clarification added)

The "thief" is often a spirit of discipline, and when it is, the "steal, kill, and destroy" usually refers to the pain and suffering it brings into your life. As I explained in Chapter 4, God doesn't *send* spirits of discipline to bring pain or suffering into our lives. Instead, it is our *sin* that gives the "thief" the legal right to act.

Do you remember the analogy I shared in Chapter 2 with the restaurant and the tow truck company, and how Jim got his car towed because he parked illegally? That's how these legal rights work. God doesn't *send* suffering into your life. But because of his spiritual laws, whenever you sin you create legal rights that invite spirits of discipline to bring the suffering to you.

The only way to get the "abundant life" that Jesus speaks about is to repent of the sins that give the thief a legal right to "steal, kill and destroy." Once you do, it removes the legal right and the torment stops.

So, even though unholy spirits don't want to serve God, they can't avoid serving him. By doing what they love to do, they actually do God's will—they bring us to repentance!

Anaphylactic shock disappears

A while back I had emailed the Prayer of Freedom to a friend of mine named Kate. She had been going through some issues I thought it might help her with.

But in a completely different turn of events, something else unexpected happened...

Mike, her husband, had been working out at the gym and drinking protein shakes every day. He kept trying different brands to see which one he liked best.

One day, he drank a shake from a new brand—one with flax seed protein—and immediately had an allergic reaction to it. He went into anaphylactic shock, his throat started closing up, and it became difficult to breathe.

Kate was scared! She was just getting him in the car to rush him to the ER when she remembered the process of the Prayer of Freedom. So she prayed—she quickly repented for sins Mike may have committed, then asked God to heal him.

Instantly, his throat opened up and he started breathing normally!

(Because the marriage covenant makes husband and wife "one," a spouse can repent on behalf of the other to help bring freedom. This means the Prayer of Freedom can be used not only for yourself, but also to help loved ones.)

Which sins created "legal rights" to your life?

How did Kate know which sins to repent of? My guess is she repented of anything she could think of, and probably did a blanket prayer, "I repent for *all* of Mike's sins." But whatever she did, it worked!

Every unrepented sin creates legal rights in the spirit realm. And it's these legal rights that allow spirits of discipline to bring suffering into your life. This includes sins you know you committed, those you don't realize you committed, things you did that you may not even consider to be sinful, and sometimes even things others did to you without your consent.

This whole world of spiritual warfare is much bigger than most people realize, and it carries far-reaching implications for the way we live. Because of that, addressing these issues often means going back and dealing with specific sins from our past—one by one—rather than relying only on broad, general prayers.

This connects with what I shared earlier about the jailer and the prisoner: the discipline and torment can only be stopped once the judgment—the jailer's "legal right"—is removed.

You don't need to remember every sin or dig through your past for this to work. God will bring to mind what matters, when it's needed.

This is simply how the Prayer of Freedom works.

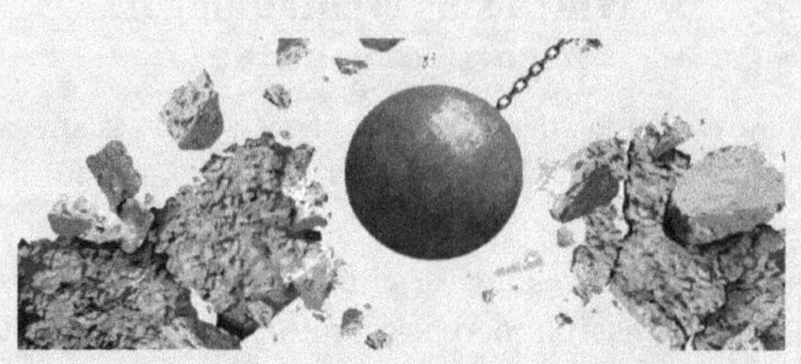

Power Prayers to Improve Your Life

Power Prayers are short, potent prayers that interrupt spiritual interference. They can give you better sleep, reduce relationship conflicts to create calmer homes, and much more. Scan the QR code (or enter the URL) to get them now.

ThePrayerOfFreedom.com/PowerPrayers

— Chapter 7 —
Sin is a cause for infirmity (Old Testament)

Before this next section, I want to pause for a moment and speak to you—not as a teacher, but as someone who understands what it's like to be hurting and looking for relief.

If you are sick, exhausted, anxious, or worn down, this book is not accusing you. Nothing you are about to read is meant to suggest you are broken, defective, or being punished. Many struggles do not begin with rebellion or willful wrongdoing, but with confusion, fear, trauma, or circumstances outside your control. God sees the whole story.

When this book speaks about sin, discipline, or repentance, it is not about condemnation. It is about removal—clearing away what does not belong so peace can return.

Repentance, as it's used here, is not self-punishment or fearful self-examination. It is simply agreeing with God about what needs to be released so freedom can take its place. You are not being asked to search your past or take responsibility for what you did not choose. God is gentle and precise.

Here's a real example of what this looks like in practice...

A friend of mine in Uganda, named John, emailed me a while back asking for money to send his sister to the doctor. She had been poisoned and desperately needed to see a specialist. Another woman in their village had also been poisoned earlier on and died, so John was extremely concerned about his sister.

God prompted me to send him the Prayer of Freedom before sending money. So I did. I told him to pray through it and get back to me within three days. If there was no change then I would send the money. Here is his email three days later, slightly adjusted for clarity and brevity...

"Greetings from Uganda,

"My sister, TJ, is a 16-year-old student studying in Level 3 of high school. As I mentioned, last month she started experiencing itching in her throat, had a terrible stomachache, and had constant headaches.

"After testing for malaria and typhoid, we took her to a medical specialist for further tests. Those tests revealed she had been poisoned! The doctor gave her an antidote, but it wasn't effective.

"By this time, TJ was unable to eat, unable to walk, bedridden, and in critical condition. It became clear she needed more intensive medical treatment. That's when I reached out to you.

"When you gave me the Prayer of Freedom, I shared it with my mother and TJ, and we all prayed it for three days as you directed us. When we did, amazing changes happened!

"TJ got her appetite back and began eating again, she was able to get out of bed and started walking again, and the stomachache completely disappeared!

"We took her back to the medical personnel for testing and after running more tests, the doctors confirmed the poison was essentially gone! All TJ needed now was an inexpensive supplement to help a little with her kidneys.

"The power of repentance made a life-changing difference in my sister's life. Thank you for sharing the Prayer of Freedom with us."

The "miracles" of the Prayer of Freedom

Because I have seen so many "miracles" God does in peoples' lives with this prayer, it has become the *first* thing I share when someone needs help in a wide range of situations—not just for health issues, but practically everything else, too.

The things we deal with—whether it's relationship conflicts, diseases like cancer, migraines, *poison*, trauma, infertility, anger, or almost anything else—while these things *could* be from purely natural causes, I have found they are often tied to a root of unrepented sin somewhere in our lives.

And what I've repeatedly seen is when people repent of specific sins, many of the problems they've been dealing with for years disappear. What's even more remarkable is when those problems involve a physical issue that doctors claim to be a normal process of aging—worn-out joints, glaucoma, arthritis, etc.—God frequently restores it all back to perfect health!

In fact, I was listening to a man speak not long ago. He uses the same process as the Prayer of Freedom and shared three case studies from his personal experience working with people who were paralyzed. In every case, after leading each person through repenting of their sins, each one was completely healed of their paralysis. One of them was even a quadriplegic who had been in a wheelchair for over a year!

If you start searching through both the Old and New Testaments, you'll see direct connections between sin and infirmity (sickness and disease). There are at least twenty direct references and as many as thirty additional, indirect references. And again, while not all infirmity is caused by sin, what's interesting is when the Bible speaks about causes of infirmities in our lives, it is almost *always* associated with sin.

Let's take a brief walk through a few passages and let Scripture show you the connection God makes between sin and infirmity—and how clearly He explains why so many are sick and suffering.

▸ Biblical link between sin and infirmity #1

Our first passage comes from the book of Numbers. As a background, this takes place after God delivered Israel out of Egypt through a man named Moses. While they are in the wilderness, Moses's siblings—Aaron and Miriam—grow jealous of the leadership role God gave him. Because they were his siblings and older than him, they challenged his position and tried to claim equal authority. Let's look at it now...

Numbers 12:1-10 – "Miriam and Aaron began to talk against Moses... "Has the LORD spoken only through Moses?" they asked. "Hasn't he also spoken through us?"... At once the LORD said to Moses, Aaron and Miriam, "Come out to the tent of meeting, all three of you." So the three of them went out. Then the LORD came down in a pillar of cloud; he stood at the entrance to the tent and summoned Aaron and Miriam. When the two of them stepped forward, he [rebuked them for their sin]... The anger of the LORD burned against them, and he left them. When the cloud lifted from above the tent, Miriam's skin was leprous—it became as white as snow. (NIV, clarifications added)

Notice what just happened — Miriam and Aaron sinned by claiming a right to the same role that God gave only to Moses. God was angry, so what did he do?

He sent a sickness upon Miriam as discipline. In other words, sin was the cause of her sickness.

▸ Biblical link between sin and infirmity #2

Now, let's look at another passage where the Bible connects sin with infirmity. This one comes from a message Moses gave to the Israelites as they prepared to enter a new land—and it's a startling one...

Deuteronomy 28:58-61—"<u>If you do not carefully follow all the words in this law</u>, which are written in this book, and do not revere this glorious and awesome Name—the Lord your God—the Lord will send fearful plagues on you and on your descendants, harsh and prolonged disasters, and <u>severe and lingering illnesses</u>. He will bring on you <u>all the diseases of Egypt</u> that you dreaded, and <u>they will cling to you</u>. The Lord will also bring on you <u>every kind of sickness and disaster</u> not recorded in this Book of the Law..." (NIV, emphasis added)

Look at the correlation here.

"If you do not carefully follow all the words of this law" means "if you disobey and sin against God."

And what happens if you sin against God?

God will send "severe and lingering illnesses. He will bring on you all the diseases of Egypt, every kind of sickness and disaster, and they will cling to you."

That means God will allow infirmity to come upon you, and that infirmity will often be chronic ("cling to you") and last a long time. And not *only* infirmity, but other kinds of disaster in your life.

Can it get any clearer? God says, "If you sin against me, I will bring all kinds of infirmity (sickness and disease) and disaster upon you that will go on and on" ... *until* you repent.

The pattern is consistent throughout Scripture: ongoing infirmity is repeatedly linked to unresolved sin.

▸ Biblical link between sin and infirmity #3

Another reference we'll look at ties in with this idea of sin 'clinging' to you. It's the story of a man named Gehazi who also gets leprosy. Let's read it now...

2 Kings 5:14-16—"So he [this is talking about a Syrian general named Naaman who had leprosy] went down and dipped himself in the Jordan seven times, as the man of God [Elisha] had told him. And his flesh was restored, and became clean like that of a young boy. Then Naaman and all his attendants went back to the man of God. He stood before him and said, 'Now I know that there is no God in all the world except in Israel. So please accept a gift from your servant.' The prophet answered, 'As surely as the Lord lives, whom I serve, I will not accept a thing.' And even though Naaman urged him, he refused." (NIV, clarification added)

Then, after Elisha refused to take Naaman's gift, Naaman heads home and goes a short distance before we pick the passage up again in verse 21...

vv. 21-26—"So Gehazi [Elisha's servant] hurried after Naaman. When Naaman saw him running towards him, he got down from the chariot to meet him. 'Is everything all right?' he asked. 'Everything is all right.' Gehazi answered. 'My master sent me to say [this is a lie, by the way], "Two young men from the company of the prophets have just come to me... Please give them a talent of silver and two sets of clothing."' 'By all means, take two talents,' said Naaman... When he [Gehazi] went in and stood before his master, Elisha asked him, 'Where have you been Gehazi?' 'Your servant didn't go anywhere,' Gehazi answered. But Elisha said to him, 'Was not my spirit with you when the man got down from his chariot to meet you? Is this the time to take money or to accept clothes—or olive groves and vineyards, or flocks and herds, or male and female slaves?'"

Now, pay attention to this final verse as Elisha continues his message to Gehazi...

v. 27—"'Naaman's leprosy will cling to you and to your descendants forever.' Then Gehazi went from Elisha's presence and his skin was leprous — it had become white as snow."

Pretty clear and direct, huh? Here we have another *very* straightforward example of sin being the root of an infirmity.

Gehazi commits a terrible sin (receiving gifts by deception for work God did, implying God's goodness could be purchased with money), and God disciplines him with sickness—in this case, leprosy that clung to him as a direct consequence of that sin.

We start to see even *clearer*, more direct references between sin and infirmity in the New Testament.

Read on. I think you'll be surprised!

— Chapter 8 —
Sin is a cause for infirmity (New Testament)

Hanna had been diagnosed with cancer. She and her husband, Jack, are devout Christians and believe in the power of God's healing miracles. So, they prayed, believing God would heal her, and he did.

God healed Hanna of cancer! And even when she went back to the doctor, *no* trace of cancer could be found. It had disappeared!

However, the doctor *still* recommended she go through chemotherapy "just in case" it started to come back. Hanna and Jack didn't want to do it, but their adult sons were concerned. They talked to the doctor, and together they pressured Hanna by saying things like, "You should still go through chemo as a back-up. It will be safer that way. We want you to do it."

Because of their insistence, Hanna began to think, "Maybe they're right. After all, you can never be too careful with cancer."

So, going against what she felt in her heart, she started the treatment. And immediately regretted it...

Two years later—

My wife and I were having lunch with my brother and his wife. He started sharing about Hanna and what has happened with her over the past couple of years.

He said, "After she went through chemotherapy, she completely changed. No longer was she that bubbly, fun and full-of-excitement woman I had known. Instead, she went into a deep, dark depression she couldn't get out of."

For the last two years, Jack had taken her to doctor after doctor, she was put on one prescription after another, and nothing worked. Jack told my brother, "Hanna is no longer the woman I married—she has *completely* changed."

When I heard her story, I recognized this as a spirit of discipline—not because she sought medical advice, but because she reversed course from what she believed God had already done. God had healed her, the doctor confirmed it, yet she turned to man as a backup out of fear the healing might not last. This was *basanizo* because the issue wasn't uncertainty, but abandoning trust in what God had done.

So, I reached out to her and ultimately led her through the Prayer of Freedom. We prayed together and she repented of having rejected God's healing and believing man's opinion instead.

Within two or three days, all her mental problems cleared up—the depression left, the anxiety and nervousness left, and "mentally" she was back to her old self again!

Hanna's story underscores, again, the direct association between sin and infirmity.

In the last chapter I promised to share more biblical passages showing that connection. So now, let's jump into the New Testament to see a few more...

▸ Biblical link between sin and infirmity #4

The previous examples I shared were from the old covenant days—the days of Israel being under the Jewish Law But what about today?

In 1 Corinthians, Paul is writing to the church in Corinth. These were Christians who believed in Jesus for salvation. However, they were a wayward church. There was a lot of sin going on—strife, jealousy, sexual immorality, and more. They were so "bad" Paul ended up writing several letters to them, admonishing and rebuking them each time, trying to correct them.

In the passage I want to share with you, Paul is instructing them on a Christian practice known as Communion or the Lord's Supper. It's a practice of sharing bread and wine as a reminder of the work Jesus did.

With that backdrop, let's pick up our verse below.

1 Corinthians 11:29-30—"For those who eat and drink [talking about taking Communion] without discerning the body of Christ, eat and drink judgment on themselves. That is why many among you are weak and sick, and a number of you have fallen asleep." (NIV, clarification and emphasis added)

When Paul says they were eating and drinking "without discerning the body of Christ," what he means is they were taking Communion in a sinful manner. As you read the rest of the text, you'll see they weren't treating it as a holy sacrament. Instead, they were treating it as a personal feast, creating division among the other believers by selfishly ignoring their needs (in those days, Communion was a full meal, not just a wafer and sip of wine or juice as many Christians do today). Because of this, they were bringing judgment on themselves.

In other words, when you take Communion, since it is a "Holy" Communion, you are to do it with a heart of love towards others, the same as Jesus did. You're not to take it in a way that excludes others and creates division, then say, "Okay God, bless me. I'm eating and drinking in remembrance of Jesus."

If you do, Paul says you are bringing judgment upon yourself because you are committing a sin when taking Communion. That's what this passage is speaking about here.

And what were the outcomes for the Corinthian *Christians* when they sinned while taking Communion?

Paul says, "That's why many among you are weak and sick, and a number of you have fallen asleep" (the term "fallen asleep" is used here as a euphemism meaning, "they have died").

So, our conclusion from this passage is the same as we've seen with all the others:

sin can be a direct cause of infirmity. And here, that infirmity manifested as weakness, sickness, and even death.

Why did God let that happen? When we look at verse 32, you'll see what I mean.

1 Corinthians 11:32—"... when we are judged in this way by the Lord, we are being disciplined <u>so that we will not be finally condemned with the world</u>." (NIV, emphasis added)

Here we see another reason for God's discipline.

It's really the same reason we discipline our own children... so something worse won't happen to them in the future. If they steal candy from their sibling, we discipline them for it. Why? So later on they won't steal bigger things from someone else and end up going to jail.

That's why God disciplines us—for our good. We know this because he tells us in **Hebrews 12:10**, "God disciplines us for our good, in order that we may share in his holiness."

But it doesn't stop there. Let's look at another example...

▶ Biblical link between sin and infirmity #5

Let's now take a quick look at another passage on what to do when you're sick. It contains a key message about healing. This passage has often caused confusion, even among Christians, so I'll pause along the way to clear up a few common misunderstandings...

James 5:14-16—"<u>Is anyone among you sick</u>? Let him call for the elders of the church, and let them pray over him, anointing him with oil in the name of the Lord. And the prayer of faith will save the one who is sick, and the Lord will raise him up. And if he has committed sins, he will be forgiven. Therefore, <u>confess your sins to one another</u> and pray for one another, <u>that you may be healed</u>..." (ESV, emphasis added)

James is being remarkably direct about the relationship between sickness and sin.

Verse 14 begins with a simple, practical question: Is anyone sick? This applies to real people dealing with real conditions—physical or mental.

Verse 15 continues: "The prayer of faith will save the one who is sick, and the Lord will raise him up." In context, James is describing restoration—being lifted out of sickness and returned to wholeness.

Then in **verse 16,** James makes the connection unmistakable:

"If he has committed sins, he will be forgiven. Therefore, confess your sins to one another and pray for one another, that you may be healed."

The connection is clear: confession—the act of repentance—precedes healing.

Now, using those short explanations, let's restate what this passage is actually saying...

"If anyone among you is sick, confess and repent of your sins so they may be forgiven and you may be healed."

James is saying it's *sin* that's causing your sickness, and if you will "confess your sins… you will be healed."

Are you starting to see a pattern with all of these passages?

The Bible is clear: sin can be a cause of infirmity. And when sin is the root of an infirmity—whether depression, panic attacks, chronic illness, or something else—repentance, expressed through confession, is the path to healing.

Taken together, these passages reveal a consistent pattern: when sin gives rise to infirmity, repentance is how freedom begins.

This framework is the backbone of the Prayer of Freedom—repenting of sins that give spirits of discipline a legal right to bring basanizo torment into your life. When those rights are removed, the discipline loses its hold, the torment stops, and freedom follows.

— Chapter 9 — Sin is still a cause for infirmity today

Since we've been looking at direct links between sin and infirmity in the Bible, it's helpful to see how these same patterns still appear today. The following stories are modern examples of what this can look like in real people's lives.

▸ Parkinson's disease disappears

A few years ago, a friend of mine named Pam worked as a hospice care provider. One of her patients, Madeline, was only forty-nine years old and dying of advanced Parkinson's disease. Doctors expected her to live no more than six weeks.

By the time Pam met her, Madeline had lost nearly all muscle control. She could barely speak and could only move the pinkie on her right hand.

While talking together, Madeline mentioned her husband had suffered from Parkinson's disease before he died—and she was diagnosed with it soon afterward. Pam, understanding the spiritual connection that can sometimes form through sexual sin, gently asked if Madeline had slept with her husband before marriage. Madeline said yes.

Pam then led her through a simple prayer of repentance and asked God to remove the Parkinson's disease.

When Pam returned the following week, Madeline was sitting up in bed, speaking clearly, and full of life. The next week, she was gone—not because she had died, but because she had improved so dramatically that hospice discharged her.

Madeline walked out of hospice less than two weeks after repenting of the sin at the root of her illness!

Encounters like this have shown me that many illnesses people struggle with can have a spiritual root of unrepented sin—and when that root is addressed, those conditions can be reversed.

▸ Addictions, migraines and more disappear

Kathryn is a young woman who had been a drug addict for years. She wrote me this message after doing the Prayer of Freedom. I have edited it for clarity and brevity...

"I want to thank you for the Prayer of Freedom. It has changed my life!

"Growing up, my relationship with my mom was really tough. She was abusive, and she and my stepdad would drink and get into lots of fights. By the time I was in seventh grade she said she didn't want anything to do with me and left. That's when life began spiraling downward. By sixteen years old I was having sex with lots of boys and started getting into drugs. That was just over 10 years ago.

"Before doing this prayer, I was addicted to heroin and fentanyl and meth. I had a lot of worry and stress and anxiety. On a scale of 1 to 10, they were probably an 8. I've had constant allergies and sinus headaches for years, migraines five out of seven days a week, and a super heavy feeling like I was carrying around an overweight backpack every day. Life has really been difficult.

"But the Prayer of Freedom and repenting changed everything. Literally, everything is gone!

"No more sinus issues. All gone. No more headaches and migraines. All gone. No more heaviness. It's all gone. No more anxiety or stress or worries. Literally, on a scale of 1 to 10, they've all gone to 0. Even my addictions have gone down to 0. I don't want drugs anymore. I have no urges for them anymore. And even the thought of any drug disgusts me. It's all gone!"

In Kathryn's case, repentance addressed what had been fueling these struggles, and the change was immediate and complete.

These stories aren't meant to be diagnostic rules, but illustrations of how repentance can bring freedom when sin lies beneath the suffering.

▸ Mental illness disappears overnight

Ashlyn is a young woman who endured severe childhood trauma and battled intense mental health challenges for much of her life. This is her story...

"I suffered from crippling anxiety, PTSD, and mental illness ever since experiencing horrific trauma from men when I was a little girl. It left me constantly afraid. Every morning, I would wake up terrified—absolutely sure something bad was going to happen. My mind never stopped racing. It was 24/7.

"Doctors had me on a heavy cocktail of medications just to function: 400mg of Seroquel, plus Buspirone, Zoloft, and sleep meds. I'd been diagnosed with bipolar disorder, borderline personality disorder, and severe anxiety. I honestly believed I'd be on medication for the rest of my life.

"Then I went through the Prayer of Freedom.

"The very next morning, I woke up—and everything was different. I wasn't afraid anymore. I wasn't terrified. For the first time since childhood, I felt peace and calm.

"When I met with my psychiatrist, she looked at me and said, "If you feel this good, you don't need the meds." So, I stopped. And I haven't needed them since. That was over six months ago.

"I can't even describe what it's like to wake up and not feel afraid. To not need medication just to get through the day. I'm free—and I never thought I would be!"

In Ashlyn's experience, once the spiritual root was addressed, the fear and torment could no longer remain. And the change wasn't gradual—it was *decisive*.

Stories like this point to the same principle: when sin plays a role in persistent suffering, repentance can be the key to breakthrough.

Why does this matter? Because understanding how these issues gain a foothold determines how they are removed. In the next chapter, we'll look at the specific ways unrepented sin creates legal rights—and how each one is addressed."

— Chapter 10 — Three types of "legal rights"

About four years ago a friend of mine handed me a phone number and asked me to pray for a seventy-three year old woman named Francis. I reached out to her, and in our phone conversation learned some fascinating things about her.

Francis was a lifelong missionary who had spent the last *fifty years* on the mission field. By all accounts, she had lived a righteous and holy life. But there was one problem.

Francis had been wheelchair-bound and unable to walk for eleven years because of extreme pain in her right foot.

When I asked her what happened, she said, "I had surgery eleven years ago because of pain in the ball of my foot. The surgery only exacerbated the problem, and the pain got worse. Since then, I've had two more surgeries on it, but the doctors couldn't correct it. So, I've been in a wheelchair ever since."

Based on everything she told me, it just felt like a spirit of discipline. So, I walked her through the steps of the Prayer of Freedom, going through a typical list of sins I've seen with most people.

"Have you ever had sex outside of marriage?" I began. "No," she replied.

"Do you have unforgiveness for anyone?" I asked. Again, she replied, "No."

"Have you ever dabbled in the occult—played with a Ouija board, participated in a séance, or anything like that?" I asked. Once again, she said, "No."

One after another, everything on my list resulted in a "No." But we needed to get to the bottom of this, so I continued, "Have you ever been part of a secret society or taken any secret oaths?" I asked. "No," she replied.

I was just about to ask the next question when Francis cut me off excitedly, "Wait! God just reminded me of a secret oath I took a long time ago. I was involved with *Rainbow Girls* in high school and took a secret oath as part of the initiation ceremony. I don't even remember what I said."

Bingo! I thought to myself. Then I said, "I think that might be it. Let's repent of that oath and see what happens."

So, I guided her through a short prayer of repentance, asked God to remove the pain, and I commanded any spirit of discipline that was there to leave immediately. When I did, all the pain in her foot instantly left! And I mean… *instantly*. It was gone. She got out of the wheelchair and started walking with NO pain.

Three months later, I checked back with her, curious to see how things were going. And she confirmed she was still walking normally—no pain, and NO wheelchair!

All it took to free her from the wheelchair was to repent of a sin—a secret, sinful oath she took over fifty years earlier.

Wow!

For Francis, the oath turned out to be an agreement that was contrary to God's will and, therefore, a sin. It's called an "agreement sin." Let's learn more about it now.

The three types of legal rights

With that, I now want to talk about the three types of "legal rights" that unrepented sin creates in our lives. And it's these legal rights that actually give spirits of discipline the authority to torment us.

Before I get into this, let me clarify one thing. I'm not asking you to analyze yourself or decide which of these apply to you. This is to help you understand how these legal rights work. When you move into Part 2, the prayer process takes care of the rest automatically. So just read, learn, and let the process do the work.

When you repent of the sin, it sets the stage to remove the legal right. But depending on what type of legal right was created determines how to remove it. And that's what I want to discuss here.

In simple terms, the three legal rights come from (1) Activity Sins, (2) Unholy Soul Ties, and (3) Agreement Sins. Let's look at them one-by-one.

Legal Right #1: Activity Sin

An activity sin is **something you do** that is contrary to God. It's usually a sin of transgression—a rebellion against what God says to do. This could be something like sex outside of marriage, harboring anger or resentment toward another person, or not forgiving someone. Many of the stories I've shared fall under this category.

In practical terms, activity sins are things **you personally do**—actions or choices that open doors, which I will show you how to address through the prayer process.

The discipline for an activity sin will continue for as long as you live. To stop the discipline from an activity sin, you must ***repent*** of the sin.

Legal Right #2: Unholy Soul Ties

The second type of legal right is what's known as an "unholy" soul tie. While this term isn't explicitly in the Bible, it is inferred. But even though it's only inferred, in practical, real-life experience, you can clearly see its existence when dealing with the Prayer of Freedom.

Unholy soul ties are not about isolated actions, but about **the people connected to those actions**—relationships through which spiritual doors were opened and may still be operating.

Unholy soul ties are a bit tricky because they involve another person in one way or another. They are formed when any sin is committed **between you and another person**. It's essentially a spiritual connection between you and the other person. This connection is a doorway which allows an unholy spirit that is working through the other person to also gain a legal right to you as well (like what happened to Madeline when she got Parkinson's disease after her husband died).

What's also unique about this type of legal right is the sin that creates the unholy soul tie does not have to be consensual. It frequently is, but it doesn't have to be. The only thing needed to create an unholy soul tie is the *presence* of sin between you and someone else.

This doesn't mean you were responsible for the sin—or that you caused what happened to you. It simply explains why spiritual effects can remain, even when the wrongdoing was not your choice.

For example, sex outside of marriage always creates an unholy soul tie with the other person. Doing drugs with someone else, or buying drugs from another person, creates an unholy soul tie with that person. But even if you did not agree to participating in the sin—maybe you were abused by someone else—simply the fact that a sin was committed against you can still create an unholy soul tie.

The issue here is not guilt. It's not even about your intentions. It's about what was opened. When sin is present between two people, something spiritual can be established—and that connection can give spirits of discipline a legal right to you.

And it's this unholy soul tie that explains why, if you've ever been in a relationship with someone who abused or controlled you, you may still feel their influence even after they're no longer in your life—even if they've passed away. That lingering control is a spirit of discipline gaining access to you through the unholy soul tie.

Unholy soul ties remain legal rights for spirits of discipline to attack until you ***break*** them.

And here's the "tricky" part about them...

Even if you repent of the sin you committed with the other person, thereby canceling that sin's legal right, the unholy soul tie still remains as a separate legal right until you *break* it as well. On top of that, unholy soul ties remain as a legal right *for as long as you live*, even if the other person has died.

The best way to explain how it works is with another story...

▸ Breaking cigarette addiction

Julie is a strong Christian and was addicted to cigarettes. She tried everything to stop smoking, but still smoked three packs of cigarettes a day. Nothing helped.

Julie had followed the precepts of the Prayer of Freedom—she repented of all the sins God reminded her of, she repented of smoking and hurting her body (God's temple), and more. But she still couldn't quit. Something was still inciting her to smoke.

Then one day while speaking with a pastor, he asked her, "Have you broken the unholy soul tie with the person who taught you to smoke?" Julie said, "No."

He then asked if she could remember who taught her how to smoke. Julie responded, "It was my babysitter from when I was ten years old. She taught me to smoke and gave me my first pack of cigarettes."

The pastor then guided her through breaking the unholy soul tie with that babysitter and asked God to remove the spirit of addiction.

He did, and Julie walked out of the pastor's office never smoking another cigarette since!

Legal Right #3: Agreement Sin

The third type of legal right is an agreement sin. This is an **agreement you make** that is contrary to God. Agreement sins are sins of iniquity—a perversion, or twisting, of God's holy standards.

Agreement sins involve **beliefs or vows you have agreed with or accepted as true**—either spoken or unspoken—that distort or twist God's truth.

Many of the problems people struggle with are tied to agreement sins. Often, those sins are tied to oaths either they or an ancestor took that was unknowingly contrary to God.

This is what happened with Francis. She wanted to join *Rainbow Girls* (a subset of an organization called *Freemasons*) because it sounded like a lot of fun. As part of the initiation ceremony, she had to repeat a secret oath. She didn't really understand what it all meant—in fact, it probably sounded a little weird at the time—but she played along and repeated it. Why? Because they were only words, right? What she didn't realize is part of that oath created an agreement sin that would come back to haunt her years later in life.

As far as the discipline goes, though, unlike an activity sin where the discipline is only directed toward you and your life, the discipline for an agreement sin continues until the agreement is broken. This means the discipline can continue for your life and be passed to your children and their children as well. What this means is some of the problems you may be dealing with could be tied to sins one of your forebearers committed.

In the Bible, it is called a sin of iniquity. And we first learn about this type of sin in the book of Exodus...

Exodus 34:7—"[God keeps] steadfast love for thousands, forgiving iniquity and transgression and sin, but who will by no means clear the guilty, visiting the iniquity of the fathers on the children and the children's children to the third and fourth generation." (ESV, clarification added)

(Just to be clear, when God says, "the iniquity of the *fathers*," he is using an all-encompassing term that means both fathers and mothers.)

This passage isn't about tracing family history—it's about understanding why patterns persist, and why they can be broken.

Did you notice this passage talks about three types of wrongdoing? One is "iniquity." Another is "transgression." And a third is "sin."

To understand what this verse is really saying, it's important to know what each of these sins are. Let's look at them in reverse order...

▸ **Sin** - In this context, "sin" refers to doing something contrary to what God wants, usually without realizing it. It's what we might call an unintentional sin—missing the mark because you didn't know better.

▸ **Transgression** - A transgression is different. It's when you know what God wants, but you choose to do something else anyway. The Bible describes this as rebellion—choosing *your* desire over God's direction. Once you know something is wrong, continuing in it moves it from unintentional sin to transgression.

James 4:17 says it this way, "Whoever knows the right thing to do and fails to do it, for him it is sin." (ESV)

Those are the first two types of "sin." But the third type is what I want to focus on to help you better understand agreement sins. This is the one that is visited from one generation to another.

▸ **Iniquity** - A sin of iniquity is a sin of perversion—it is a twisting of God's holy standard into something it was never meant to be. Rather than simply disobeying God, iniquity reshapes what God declared good, normal, or sacred into a distorted version of itself.

This is why iniquity is different from *sin* or *transgression*. It is not just about an action, but about agreeing with a false version of God's design... and then living from that agreement.

Because it is rooted in agreement, iniquity can pass from one generation to another until it is renounced. This doesn't mean you committed the original act—it means the agreement behind it continued.

Here's a simple way to see the difference. Sleeping with someone outside of marriage is a transgression—you know God's standard, but you choose to violate it. But iniquity goes deeper than behavior. It happens when God's standard itself is *reshaped*—when what He calls holy is treated as unholy, or what He forbids is affirmed as good.

This can show up in many ways, including sexual behavior, identity, power, authority, or any area where God's design is redefined or reversed. The issue is no longer just behavior, but a twisted standard that people begin to accept as normal or true.

This is why iniquity carries generational weight. When a twisted standard is accepted and lived out, it creates an agreement that can continue affecting future generations—even when they don't understand where it began. Once that agreement is identified and renounced, the discipline attached to it no longer has a legal right to continue.

Other sins of iniquity we frequently see today are things like adultery (twisting God's holy standard of marriage), addictions, some forms of abuse, all forms of witchcraft, and more.

I share these simply to illustrate what iniquity can look like when something God designed is fundamentally reshaped and acted out through agreement.

The term "generational curse" people talk about is often a spirit of discipline tied to a sin of iniquity that comes down through the generations. It may look like a pattern of sickness from generation to generation, or abusiveness, or addiction, or anything else. Whatever it looks like, you may start seeing it in your children, too. And it may continue down through the generations *until* that sin is repented of.

And as a reminder, just like with all spirits of discipline, it seems God allows them in your life *because* he loves you and wants to bring about repentance.

God wants that sin repented of. And once you repent of it (even if it was committed by a parent or grandparent), the discipline (the "curse") goes away. That's basically the "big idea" of our passage in Exodus.

(Before I explain this further, I want to ease a concern you might be feeling. Nothing I'm describing here means you are being blamed for something you didn't choose or even know about. This is not about fault—it's about why something may be operating in your life, and why it can now be stopped.)

This is what God means in **Exodus 34:7** when he says, "I will visit the iniquity of the fathers to the third and fourth generation."

But what does it mean to "visit" a sin on future generations?

Well, I've already alluded to it—it typically appears as a spirit of discipline in the form of torment that carries down through our family generations. That's the *basanizo* I mentioned earlier. Addictions coming down, divorce coming down, abuse coming down, sickness coming down, broken relationships coming down, early deaths coming down—we see these patterns, and they all have to do with iniquity.

You don't have to explain or prove any of this. Simply noticing a pattern is enough.

Suffice it to say, even if someone else committed the original sin, it can still belong to you from a "legal rights" standpoint and open the door to a spirit of discipline. Scripture refers to this as being *imputed*—their action is counted to you, not because you committed it, but because it continues through you (cf. **Hebrews 7:9**).

This doesn't mean you are guilty of the original act. It means you now have the authority to repent of what has been continuing—and when you do, the discipline stops in your life and no longer passes on to your children.

More precisely, when discipline comes through an "agreement sin," freedom involves more than repentance alone. The agreement itself must also be ***renounced***—and the Prayer of Freedom guides you through that automatically.

At the root, every agreement sin is simply believing something contrary to God's holy standard. Because you believe it, you agree with it. And because you agree with it, you act on it—twisting what God intended into something it was never meant to be.

▸ Patterns of discipline

Discipline from agreement sins is usually easy to recognize, especially if it was something one of your ancestors did. All you have to do is look for patterns, either in your life or coming down through your family line. The pattern you're looking for is usually some form of destruction or illness. If you see this type of pattern, there's a good chance a spirit of discipline is behind it, tied to an agreement sin.

For example, addiction is a *big* pattern you'll see. When I work with people struggling with addictions, I'll ask them to raise their hands if their parents or grandparents struggled with addictions as well. And guess what—80% of them raise their hands! Addiction is often a spirit of discipline tied to an agreement sin. That means if you want to get rid of the addiction, you must first renounce the agreement.

But addiction is just one of many patterns you'll find. Other patterns may be abuse, divorce, anxiety, asthma, cancer, early death, suicide, and more. Doctors will typically say, "You are genetically *pre-disposed* to such-and such an issue," but they are only looking at it from a physical perspective. On a spiritual level, you'll often find the *true* source of the issue is an unrepented sin, and in this case, an agreement sin.

How do I know?

Because the Prayer of Freedom will often get rid of those issues. And if it *does*, it's because it was a spirit of discipline.

▸ My own battle with Agreement Sins—from 150 years ago!

For many years, something in my life didn't make sense. I could build my business, see it succeed, and then—without a clear reason—it would collapse. This cycle repeated again and again, until it felt like someone was actively working against everything I did.

Eventually, through prayer and with help from someone experienced in these issues, God revealed that what I was dealing with wasn't random or personal failure—it was a spirit of discipline tied to an agreement sin in my family line.

The sin traced back more than 150 years to my great-great-great-grandfather and the sin of slavery—an injustice so serious that Scripture treats it as an iniquity. Once we identified it, I repented of it, renounced the agreement tied to it, and asked God to remove the discipline.

Within months, everything changed. What had felt like constant resistance lifted, and my life moved from pressure and instability to peace and forward momentum.

That's when I knew this process works—not just for obvious sins, but for hidden roots you would never think to look for on your own.

▸ Secret societies and secret oaths

Some generational agreement sins begin with oaths, pledges, or ritual statements made by someone in a family line—sometimes knowingly, and sometimes without understanding their spiritual implications. This can occur in organizations that require oaths of secrecy (such as Freemasonry, Shriners, Eastern Star, and others). Many people join for fellowship, service, business connections, or charitable work—and those motivations are not the issue. The concern is not the people or the relationships, but the nature of certain oaths themselves.

In many oath-based organizations, members are asked to repeat phrases or symbolic commitments without closely examining their meaning—often assuming they are ceremonial, exaggerated, or "not meant literally." From a spiritual standpoint, however, agreeing aloud to statements involving **absolute loyalty, secrecy under penalty, generational obligation, or undefined spiritual allegiance** can still function as real agreements, even when no harm was intended. If this applies to you, don't get stuck or defensive here. You don't need to analyze specific wording or judge past decisions. The goal is simple awareness. If you know of personal or ancestral involvement—or even feel uncertain—you'll have a place to note it later in Part 2. The Prayer of Freedom is designed to address both known and unknown agreement sins, including those connected to past or present oaths.

Before moving forward, let me relieve a burden you may be feeling. You are not expected to diagnose yourself, place yourself in the right category, or untangle the full history of every issue in your life. The purpose of this chapter isn't to assign labels, but to give *orientation*—to help you understand the landscape on how spiritual issues commonly enter and operate.

The Prayer of Freedom doesn't require you to figure everything out. It simply requires you to be willing, honest, and responsive as you move forward.

As you enter the next section, don't try to hold all of this together in your mind. The process is guided step by step, bringing forward whatever God wants you to address at this time. What matters most is not how much you understand, but simply your willingness to begin.

Before you move on, if someone close to you comes to mind—spouse, child, parent, or friend—**write their name down.**

Later, I'll show you a simple way to help them walk through this process to freedom.

Recap

Before closing out this chapter, let's recap a few things…

First, activity sins are things you *do*, and to stop the discipline you **repent** of the sin.

Second, unholy soul ties are spiritual connections created between you and another person when sin is committed *between* the two of you, and to stop the discipline you **break** the soul tie.

Third, agreement sins are things you (or someone in your family line) *agreed to*, and to stop the discipline you **renounce** the agreement.

Each of these gives spirits of discipline a legal right to operate. What differs is not whether freedom is possible, but how their right is removed—and the Prayer of Freedom is designed to address all three.

That discipline most often shows up as *basanizo*—physical suffering, mental suffering, or physical pain. But it can also take other forms, including abusiveness from others, addictions, repeated failure in work or relationships, economic destruction (as happened with me), and more.

Because these patterns often persist over time, they point to something deeper than circumstance alone—and that's what this chapter is helping you recognize.

Regardless of the form of the discipline, God set up the spiritual laws that allow the discipline to happen for a reason—because he loves you and wants you to repent of your sin so you can conform more to his image and the image of his Son.

The reason this matters—and the reason I've shared so many stories throughout this book—is not to overwhelm you, but to **give you hope**. Every testimony you've read involved someone who was stuck, confused, or out of options. Then, once the spiritual root was removed through the Prayer of Freedom, *everything* changed.

If you've been struggling with things that just don't make sense and you can't seem to get rid of them—fibromyalgia, arthritis, headaches, sickness, heaviness, rage, relationship failures, work or career failures, whatever it is—when a problem becomes chronic and won't lift, it often points to a spiritual root rather than just circumstances.

Ready for a change?

If you struggle to believe all of this—if it sounds too good to be true or too simple to handle your problems—that's okay. Just don't let it stop you from doing the prayer. You don't have to believe it for God to bring freedom to your life. You just have to repent. So, try it. You have nothing to lose… and a life of freedom to gain!

And to give you encouragement, I want to share the testimony and issue grid from Bernice. She was one of my students where I volunteer teach, and her results are encouraging to see.

The main thing I want you to see is how, after her first week, very little changed in her life. But by the fourth week, the problems she had been struggling with had almost completely melted away and she felt like a new person. And within a few more weeks of doing the Prayer of Freedom, I believe most everything on her list will have completely disappeared.

Here's her story, edited slightly for clarity…

Bernice's story

"I had many unrepented sins and unholy soul ties from the time I was a child to today, everything from sexual abuse as a child to many others. And I've been suffering with all kinds of aches and pains in my body.

By the time I started the Prayer of Freedom, my life felt overwhelming, with problems stacked on top of problems.

"I had been diagnosed with multiple mental health conditions and struggled with addiction and serious medical issues. My life had been in a downward spiral for a very long time. That's where I was when you shared the Prayer of Freedom with me.

"When I started doing the prayers, I didn't feel much of a difference in anything. For the first week, it seemed like nothing was changing.

"But then, **as the days and weeks passed, I could feel things starting to change.** The thoughts in my head were more of God, and a soothing peace of mind started to flood over me.

"I'm still working on some of these, but for the most part I feel completely different. I feel so much lighter, like a brand new person!

"Thank you, Mr. Carmichael, for teaching me this method."

While her story shares a lot of what's been going on in her life, when you look at her issue grid (similar to what you'll find in Chapter 11) you'll see how much she had been dealing with. You'll also see how powerful the Prayer of Freedom has been in melting it all away!

Bernice's issue grid

Issue	Scale of 0-10, with 10 = worse		
	BEFORE the Prayer	AFTER 1 Week	AFTER 4 Weeks
Heaviness (feels like you are carrying around a heavy backpack every day)	10	8	2
Darkness (seems like your mind or life is dark)	10	↓	2
Mental torments (list below, such as depression, anxiety, voices in head, etc)	10		2
bypolar type 1 and 2	10	9	2
depression	10	↓	3
anxiety	10		3
Voicees in my head	10		3
Mom and Dad / Youth Min	10		3
Pain or Stiffness (list below what type of pain or stiffness, such as back pain, chest pain, stiff left knee, etc)	10	↓	3
Block artiries in my fa	10		3
Arthuritis in both hips	10	9	3
Knee pain	10	↓	2
Back pain	10		3
restless leg	10		
Sicknesses / Illnesses (list below what type, such as asthma, allergies, bipolar, etc)	10		3
bipolar	10	9	4
Copd	10	↓	4
Nueropathy	10		3
RLS	10		2
Addiction (list below any addictions you suffer with, such as drugs, alcohol, pornography, etc)	Rate the level of your urges		
drugs	0	6	0
pornography	10	8	0
Cigaretts	10	10	10

Hopefully, your life hasn't been as difficult as Bernice's. Her life is an extreme example and she's had lots of problems to deal with. But the good news is: if the Prayer of Freedom can free her from *her* problems, it can free you from *yours*, too!

If you are ready for a change—ready to get free of whatever issues are in your life—then the time has come. Take the next step and start the Prayer of Freedom process for yourself.

In Part 2, we'll start looking at the Prayer of Freedom and how to apply it. And not only how to do it for yourself, but how you can pray it on behalf of your children, spouse, and even parents, to help set them free.

With that orientation in place, we're now ready to move from understanding what's been happening to taking the first steps toward freedom.

So, if you (or a child, spouse, or parent) suffer with health issues, relationship conflicts, emotional pain, psychological trauma, addictions, or any other life challenge, there may be a root of unrepented sin at its core. And if there is, freedom *is* possible!

Let's begin…

– Part 2 –

Field Manual

Stepping Into Freedom

The best place to begin stepping into freedom is with the Simplified Prayer below. It's a short, high-impact way to invite God to start clearing away spiritual clutter and move you toward deeper freedom. You do not need to feel fully prepared to begin. When you're ready, pray the following out loud. A quiet whisper is enough.

▸ *Simplified Prayer* ◂

(pray out loud)

"God, I repent of my sins. I want freedom from (list any issues you want freedom from) and I ask you to help me. I know I don't have to remember everything right now. So, please remind me of any sin I need to repent of or person I need to forgive to set me free.

Unforgiveness: "I repent of unforgiveness, for I know that it is a sin. I therefore choose to forgive, release all judgments against, and break all unholy soul ties with the following people: (list their names).

Sexual sin (*any sexual activity outside of marriage*): "I repent of my sexual sins with the following people, I break all unholy blood contracts with each one, and I renounce and break all unholy soul ties with them, including: (list their names). I break all unholy soul ties with their sexual partners and all my other sexual partners I may not recall. I also break all unholy soul ties with any who encouraged me to engage in these sexual activities, including: (list their names).

Occult (*Quija board, séance, etc*)**:** "I repent of and renounce all occult activity I have engaged in, including (list any occult activity), and I break all unholy soul ties with those who encouraged me to do those activities, including (list their names).

Other sins: "I also repent of (list any other sins God reminds you of), and I break all unholy soul ties with (list anyone's name you did those sins with).

"And now, in the authority of God, I command every unholy spirit to leave me immediately. I declare you have no further right to me, and I command you to go *now*, in God's name, and go where God tells you to go.

"I also speak to the spirit of (name your issue, for example "back pain") and I command you to go as well. Go now, in God's name. (*if you have multiple issues you're dealing with, address them one at a time*)

"God, I now ask that you enforce my freedom. I ask that you remove all unholy spirits from my life right now and set me free. Amen!"

If you just prayed that and felt a shift—peace, lightness, even tears—that's a sign that something in the spiritual realm is starting to break. If you didn't feel anything, that's okay too—many people don't at first. Progress is not measured by sensation. The full prayer process ahead goes much deeper. Either way, you've taken an important step.

With that said, if you came here from Chapter 1 and you're ready to keep learning, return to Chapter 2 now. But if you started your journey here in Part 2, simply continue to go deeper into the full Prayer of Freedom. The next sections don't depend on whether you feel any change yet from the prayer you just prayed.

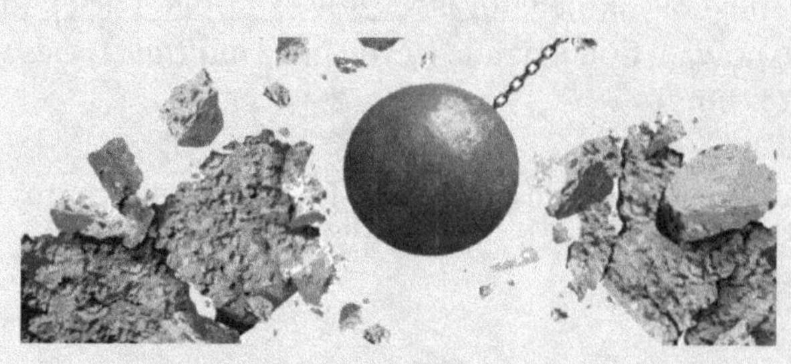

Download Our Mobile App

We've created an interactive mobile app for use with the next section. It will help you more effectively gain freedom from your challenges. Download from your App or Play store (search "Get Radical Faith"), or scan the QR code (or enter the URL) to go directly there now.

— Chapter 11 —
The first steps to breaking free

Now, let's talk about the Prayer of Freedom. In just a moment, I'm going to share it with you and teach you how to use it. Before I do, though, you need to understand that it is most effective—though not required—when you have personally entrusted yourself to Jesus and His renewing work. Scripture calls this becoming a "new creation" in Christ—turning from sin and trusting Him to save and transform us.

That means you've confessed being a sinner and believe in Christ Jesus for salvation. If this is already familiar to you, simply keep going. This isn't about religion—it's about relationship. Believing in Jesus doesn't mean you have to join a religion or follow a set of rules. It simply means you're choosing to trust the one who came to set you free If you're still considering this, you don't need to sort it all out right now to keep reading.

In case you don't know much about who Jesus is, let me share what the Bible tells us about him.

In simple terms, the Bible tells us that all of us have sinned and fall short of God's glory. That's what I meant earlier when I said, "sin breaks the relationship with God" and "sin breaks the image of God."

However, because God loves us beyond measure, and because we can never fully pay the penalty for our sin, God sent His Son, Jesus, to pay it in our place. Instead of carrying the burden of fixing ourselves or trying to reach freedom through our own effort, Jesus does for us what our own discipline and striving could never achieve. He gives us the transformation we could never earn.

Here's how the Bible says it in **John 3:16–17** (paraphrased): "God loved us so much that He gave His only Son, Jesus, so that whoever believes in Him will not perish but have eternal life. For God did not send His Son into the world to condemn us for our sins, but to save us through Him."

That happened about 2,000 years ago. Jesus was a person just like you and me except for two things: he was completely sinless, and he was fully God.

Jesus even tells us why he came in **Luke 4:18** (paraphrased). He said it was "to proclaim good news to the poor, to proclaim freedom for the prisoners, recovery of sight for the blind, and to set the oppressed free." In other words, everything I've been sharing about.

How did Jesus do that?

He lived a perfect life, never sinning even one time. Then, he was crucified on a cross (a Roman method of execution) and died. **God used his death—the death of**

God's sinless Son—as a sacrifice to pay the penalty for our sins in our place. The Bible says he "bore our sins in his body on the cross, so that we might die to sin and live for righteousness." (**1 Peter 2:24**, NIV)

After he died, he was buried. Then, three days later he came back to life and rose from the grave, proving that death had no power over him and showing that he has the power to free us from eternal death, too. Today, he sits in heaven with God.

Jesus did all of that for you and me—to pay the penalty for our sins so we no longer carry the burden of completing the spiritual journey by our own strength. God offers this gift freely, but we only receive what Jesus accomplished when we trust in Him and His sacrifice on our behalf.

The Bible says, "Believe in the Lord Jesus and you shall be saved" (Acts 16:31, paraphrased).

In this context, "saved" means being rescued from the endless effort of trying to purify yourself, elevate your inner state, or reach peace through your own strength. Instead, God gives the peace and eternal life we could never earn, as a gift through Jesus.

Again, this isn't about joining a religion. It's about making a personal choice to enter into a relationship with the one who gave his life for you.

So, if you have never made a personal commitment to Jesus by confessing you are a sinner and believing in him to receive salvation, and you would like to be that "new creation" in Christ Jesus, then all you have to do is pray a simple prayer like this...

"Jesus, I confess I'm a sinner. I repent of my sins. Please forgive me. I want your freedom and new life. Please come into my life right now. I surrender it to you and choose to follow you as my Lord. Amen."

That's it—just a simple, heartfelt prayer. It's not the words themselves that matter, but the decision being expressed through them.

If you prayed that sincerely and opened your heart to Jesus, Scripture teaches that He begins the work of making you a "new creation" in Him. That work does not depend on what you feel in the moment. Some people notice peace or relief right away; others do not—and both are normal. What matters is what has been set in motion, not what you can sense yet.

So, if this prayer reflects your choice, you have taken an important step forward.

Now, let's talk about the Prayer of Freedom. There are a few more things to understand before I share the prayer itself...

How fast will this work?

People often ask, "How fast will the Prayer of Freedom work?" My response is always, "It depends." That doesn't mean it's uncertain—it means the timing isn't the same for everyone.

I've seen some get freedom from their issues in one day. For others, it may take a week, a month, or possibly longer, depending on what's involved. Neither outcome means something is wrong.

What I've learned with this process is if your issues are rooted in unrepented sin, then once you repent of those sins and ask God to remove the spirits of discipline, they will leave. This isn't something you have to worry about messing up. That's why my greatest encouragement as you go through this process is to remain patient, be persistent, and allow it to unfold without trying to measure it too early.

Making the Prayer of Freedom work for YOU

While I don't fully understand why some issues take longer than others to disappear, my experience is it often relates to three conditions that allow the Prayer of Freedom to work as intended. These aren't techniques to master, but conditions that let the process do what it's designed to do. When they're in place, it tends to work more effectively.

First, pray the Prayer of Freedom *aloud*. Spirits of discipline need to know you've repented of the sins giving them legal access to you. Since they can't hear your thoughts, speaking aloud lets them hear your voice. You don't need to speak loudly—spirits hear well, so a soft whisper is sufficient.

Second, you must engage the Prayer of Freedom with a heart of repentance. Simply reading the words but it's not from your heart won't bring results. It's not the words themselves, but the attitude of your heart, guided by the words, that makes it effective. When repentance is present, the Prayer of Freedom will work for you.

Third, you must repent of the specific sins that give spirits of discipline a legal right to you. If you miss the sins for which you are being disciplined, the discipline won't go away. This is why honesty matters more than memory. So be thorough when making your lists, starting with what you remember and trusting God to bring the rest to mind as needed.

Instructions on using our app

If you downloaded our mobile app from the page just prior to the beginning of this chapter, I now want to share how to use it. If you did not download it, you can find it in your App Store or Google Play Store by searching for *Get Radical Faith*.

Once you open the app, I encourage you to tap the top button labeled "**Watch This First.**" It's a short video that explains how to best use the app to get the most from my training videos.

From this point forward, I'll periodically reference specific training videos on the app to provide greater clarity and instructions on certain topics.

Anytime you see our app's logo and video title (see example below), if you want to learn more on that topic, pause for a moment, select *The Prayer of Freedom* button on the home page of our app, then watch the specific training being referenced.

If you've been dealing with deep, painful, or long-standing struggles, it's important to watch each video as it's introduced. These videos explain *why* the steps matter and help you understand the deeper parts of the process. For many people, that understanding is what allows the process to unfold more smoothly and leads to lasting freedom.

Please note: these videos are available only through our app and not online.

[video description here]

Spiritual opposition

Once you start the Prayer of Freedom process, it's not uncommon for new or unexpected issues to surface or intensify for a short time in your life. If this happens, what's going on is the unholy spirits tormenting you are pushing back as you are trying to remove them. They may create problems or distractions to pull your attention away from completing the process.

I don't want to alarm you, but I do want you to be informed. As you start going through this process, if you suddenly feel attacked with pain, sickness, or difficult life issues, it's often a sign that the process is working. Nothing is wrong with you. If those things happen, stay steady and continue. Don't let worry take over, and don't let these things stop you.

Because of this kind of resistance, I encourage you to find one or two friends to pray for you—what we sometimes call a prayer buddy—once or twice daily as you go through the Prayer of Freedom. We've found this can greatly help reduce that oppression.

If you don't have anyone you can ask, join *The Prayer of Freedom Community* (**ThePrayerOfFreedom.com/Communit**y) where you can connect with others. We have a Prayer & Support Channel where people request prayer and connect with others who need prayer in return. Praying for each other helps everyone stay steady and continue moving forward.

So how should they pray for you? I suggest giving them the "Beginning Prayer" you'll see in Chapter 12 and have them pray it over you twice daily.

Watch this training to learn more about spiritual opposition.

Chapter 11: Spiritual opposition when doing the prayers

The structure of the prayer process

The structure of the prayer has been carefully designed for specific reasons. It's the combination of each prayer and the number of times you pray it that makes the process most effective in setting you free. This isn't about earning results—it's about fully closing the doors that have been opened.

Sometimes, people try to shortcut the process by skipping certain prayer sections or praying them fewer times than recommended. In my experience, when you skip steps, you often miss out on the full results. Not because the prayer failed, but because the process wasn't completed.

And if you come from a Christian background where repetition in prayer raises questions, you may already recognize this concern. I address it more fully in the "For Christian Friends" section in the Appendix and in a short teaching video that explains the biblical reasoning behind this structure. This isn't repetition for repetition's sake, and it isn't about persuading God—it's about completing the process with understanding and confidence. If this gives you pause, I encourage you to review that material before moving forward. Here's the video:

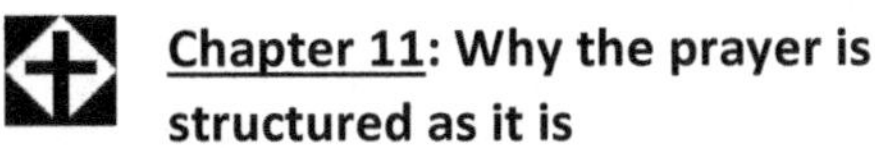

Chapter 11: Why the prayer is
structured as it is

Instructions

We're almost there! Before you start praying the Prayer of Freedom, I encourage you to make a list of all the issues in your life and rate each one on an intensity scale of 0 to 10 (10 being the highest). Then, after completing the Prayer of Freedom, review your list and re-rate the intensity of each item. This will be a great encouragement to you as you see what God does in your life. I have included a grid on the next page for you to make your list.

And because agreement sins from your life (or those of your ancestors) may also be impacting your children, I have included a second grid to complete on their behalf as well. This will help you measure the overflow impact the Prayer of Freedom has on *their* lives when those agreement sins are renounced.

Once you complete the following issue grids, then continue to the next chapter and begin the Prayer of Freedom.

What Happens Next

Chapter 12 walks you step by step through the actual Prayer of Freedom. **Chapter 13** shows how to use this process to help others. **Chapter 14** explains what to do if issues still remain after going through the process and how to maintain your freedom long term. Then **Chapter 15** shows how to help set loved ones free, even if they can't or aren't willing to do this on their own.

Also, as you move into the Prayer of Freedom, you don't have to walk through this process alone. We have created *The Prayer of Freedom Community* for those who have questions while working through it, want someone to pray for them as they do, or simply want to be around others who understand what this journey looks like. You'll also find frequent live Q&A calls and other resources to help you understand even more as you move forward.

To learn more, go to **ThePrayerOfFreedom.com** and select **Community** from the menu, or scan the QR code below:

But for now, simply continue to Chapter 12 and begin.

Issue grid for YOU

Before you began this book, you likely had a number of struggles—such as depression, addiction, anxiety, anger, relationship conflicts, pain, etc. Even though many issues may have already cleared after praying the Simplified Prayer in Chapter One, list everything you've dealt with, and their intensity level, before starting this book. After completing Prayer #2 sessions, re-rate the items. Then again after Prayer #3 sessions. This will show you what God has done and encourage others you share it with.

Scale 0 to 10 (10 = highest)

Issue	Before Praying	After 3 days Prayer 2	After 30 days Prayer 3

Issue grid for your CHILDREN

Make a list of everything your children struggle with, including behavior issues, and rate each one. This grid will help you see the impact to their lives when you remove generational sins from your life with the Prayer of Freedom. For example, one woman I worked with had two daughters who suffered with severe asthma. After finishing the Prayer of Freedom, their asthma instantly disappeared—it was a generational torment tied to their mother's sin.

Scale 0 to 10 (10 = highest)

Child's Name and Issue	Before Praying	After 3 days Prayer 2	After 30 days Prayer 3

— Chapter 12 —
Prayer of Freedom

Now it's time to start! You don't need to feel ready, confident, or fully prepared to begin. Begin by working through the **List Preparation Guide** below, then immediately following it is the Prayer of Freedom that sets you free.

If you've tried things before and they didn't work, it's normal to feel cautious. And if part of you is thinking, "How could repentance possibly change all this?"—that's okay, too. You don't have to feel hopeful, and you don't have to fully believe for this to work. Just give it a chance. Take it one step at a time and bring your honesty to God—He can meet you wherever you are.

The List Preparation Guide is a process that walks you through various categories where you might have unrepented sins. It's like a "memory jogger" to help you remember things over time—not something you must complete perfectly before you can move forward.

Additionally, as you create your lists, you'll be doing it in partnership with God, asking Him to bring to mind what needs to be addressed. You don't need to remember everything at once—just write down what comes to mind. If something truly matters, God will surface it at the right time. Your role is simply to begin; God will bring to mind what needs to be addressed—sometimes now, and sometimes later as you continue.

Also, if attention is difficult, just do one list at a time and work it in short sessions. Here's how:

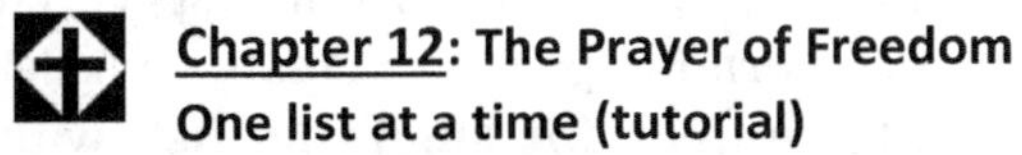

Chapter 12: The Prayer of Freedom
One list at a time (tutorial)

List Preparation Guide

(list unrepented sins by category)

The key to being set free starts with thoroughly and accurately completing each category in the List Preparation Guide. **This is the most important step in the entire process** because anything left off your list will not be addressed in the prayer—and may continue to affect you until it is addressed later. So, take your time and be thorough.

To help, I've recorded short teaching sessions in our app for each category in the list. These brief videos explain what each category means and what types of things to include. I highly recommend watching the training for each item so you fully understand its spiritual impact and know what to include on your list.

As you work through each category, use the following two prayers:

▸ Beginning Prayer ◂

Pray *before* making your lists, and pray out loud (this invites God to guide you and blocks spiritual interference as you begin making your lists)

"Lord, I ask you to remind me of every sin and person I need to include on my lists to be set free. And in Jesus' name, I bind every unholy spirit and command you down. And during the entire time I am making my lists and doing the prayers, I forbid any of you, in Jesus's name, to manifest, distract, confuse, or in any other way attempt to prevent me from doing either, and I declare all your works against me to be ineffective."

▸ Ending Prayer ◂

Pray *after* completing each category list (this ensures nothing important is missed before moving on to the next category)

"Lord, I have now completed this list in full. If there is anything or anyone else I need to add, please bring it to my mind now."

(then wait two or three minutes. If God brings something or someone to your attention, add it to your list. Before moving on to the next category, **repeat this prayer** and wait again until nothing else comes to mind. This is a crucial step to get the best results—so don't rush it.)

Create your lists in the spaces provided in this book. If you run out of space, either use the blank pages at the end of the book as "overflow" pages, or create your lists in your phone, computer or a notebook. Be sure to **number and label your lists** with the same number and labels as below. The Prayer of Freedom references different lists to pray through at different times, so having your lists numbered and labeled properly will make it much easier to do.

Grab a pen and work through each list carefully, one at a time. After you complete each list, pray the **Ending Prayer** above before moving on. That prayer matters—it invites God to bring to mind anything you missed. And remember: the Prayer of Freedom is most effective when your lists are as thorough as you can make them *right now*. Don't rush. Give God space to bring to mind anything important that needs to be addressed.

As you work through these categories, not every section will apply to you. Simply notice whether each category resonates. If it does, complete that section. If not, move on. Don't force memories—just work with what naturally comes to mind.

When you've worked through the lists and feel they are reasonably complete, you're ready to move forward and begin praying through the Prayer of Freedom that follows.

Before you begin, take this **one step at a time.** You don't have to work through all categories at once. This process is meant to be done slowly—one list at a time, in the order they're given here, and focus only on the category in front of you right now.

There is no race here, so don't rush. Most of the things you're dealing with didn't start overnight, and you don't need to force this process into a single sitting. Simply work through this list, complete it as best you can, and then move on when you're ready. Steady is better than fast.

You may be surprised how naturally the right things come to mind as you move through the lists. Trust that process. If something important needs attention, God usually brings it to the surface at the right time.

#1 Parent Relationship

Our early childhood experiences dramatically shape our life as we grow up. For example, if a parent or grandparent abused or abandoned you as a child, it can affect how you later relate to God, sometimes creating bitterness toward Him. Even if you had a "great" childhood but had to assume adult responsibilities due to a parent's absence—whether through abandonment, divorce, death, military deployment, or chronic illness—this, too, can impact your life today. Both parental actions and life circumstances can unconsciously create wounds that foster unforgiveness toward parents, which can open the door to significant torment later in life. As you work through this section, remember there is no need to force memories or emotions.

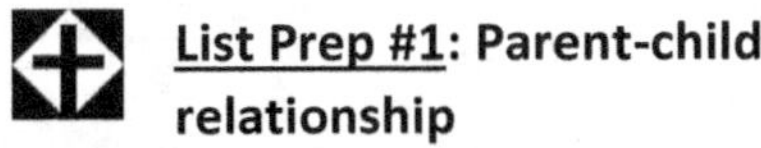

Action Item: create a separate list for *each* parent (one for father, one for mother, and one for grandparent). List all issues, events, traumas, abuse, rejection or actions that involved you, either directly or indirectly. These could include: "abandonment due to prolonged illness" (where you had to shoulder their responsibilities), "arguments and alcohol drinking," or any negative actions that led you to make internal vows against being like them (ex. "I will not drink like my mother"), and so on. Write down what comes to mind naturally—don't strain to remember everything at once. To help identify all issues, think through each age group of childhood separately—(**1**) less than 5 years old, (**2**) between 5 and 7 years old, (**3**) between 8 and 13 years old, (**4**) above 13 years old—and list all things that come to mind. If nothing comes up for a particular age range, that's okay—just move on.

Father: ____

____

____

____

____

____

____

Mother: ____

____

____

____

____

____

____

Grandparent: ____

____

____

____

____

#2 Unforgiveness

Unforgiveness often leads to significant torment in people's lives. Forgiveness is a choice rather than an emotion. It involves *choosing* to forgive someone who has harmed you. Forgiveness does not require you to reconcile with that person nor allow that person back into your life. It is a one-sided action that *you* do. Forgiveness does not mean you agree with what that person did to you. It merely means you release your judgment against that person and free them from your heart so *you* can be freed from *basanizo* torment. This is about release, not justification. Watch the training to learn how to more easily forgive.

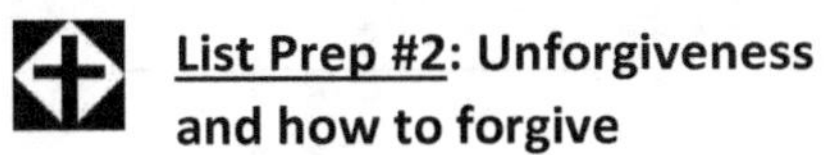

List Prep #2: Unforgiveness and how to forgive

Action Item: make a list of everyone who has hurt you—either directly against you or indirectly against a loved one—whether they are still living or dead (include yourself if you have unforgiveness toward yourself), then list every hurt they did to you. You don't need to soften or explain what happened. Simply name it honestly and move on.

#3 Sexual Sin

Sexual sin is *any* sexual act you do outside of marriage. This section is about honesty, not self-condemnation.

List Prep #3: Sexual sin

Action Item: make a list of **(1)** everyone with whom you have engaged in *any* sexual activity outside of marriage—including if you had sexual activity with your spouse before you married, or any sex with animals (bestiality); and **(2)** any other person who may have encouraged you to do that activity (such as a friend urging you to "do it"). You are **not** being asked to relive events or analyze motives—only to name what occurred. If you do not remember their name, simply write a brief description (ex. "the guy with the blue hat" or "the girl at the pool party"). If details feel unclear, write what you can and move on. God will surface anything else that needs to be addressed later.

#4 Generational Sins

In the Old Testament, God states he will visit the iniquities of fathers and mothers upon the third and fourth generations. Iniquities are grave sins that are passed down through the bloodline, meaning you inherit them from your parents. They act as open doors for tormenting spirits to attack you and are sometimes referred to as "generational curses." These sins frequently create recurring issues coming down your ancestral lineage. Examples of generational sins (and the torment that visits future generations) include **abortion, abuse, addiction, adultery, anger, anxiety, divorce, murder, suicide, rage, violence,** and more. Ancestral involvement in practices like **witchcraft, secret societies, occult, divination, or slavery** also create generational sins. Another increasingly prevalent form of generational sin is "unclean conception" (you or an ancestor being conceived by sex outside of the marriage through fornication, rape, etc).

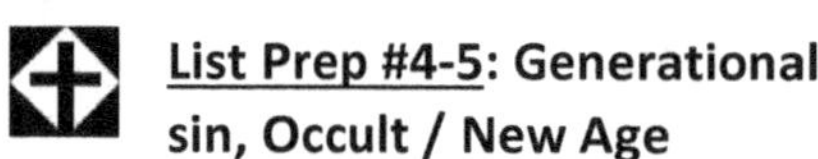

List Prep #4-5: Generational
sin, Occult / New Age

Action Item: make a list of every generational sin you are aware of in your ancestry (including if you or an ancestor had an "unclean conception"), any patterns of sin you see coming down through the generations, and any occult-type sin (see list in #5 below) you know of. You don't have to research your family history or uncover everything at once. List what you are aware of right now. If something is unknown or uncertain, simply leave it for now.

____

____

____

____

____

#5 Occult

Engaging in occult activities can give tormenting spirits a legal right to your life. Jesus says in **John 10:1–2**, "Truly, truly, I say to you, he who does not enter the sheepfold [i.e. spiritual realm] by the door but climbs in by another way, that man is a thief and a robber. But he who enters by the door is the shepherd of the sheep." In this passage—and again in **John 10:9**—Jesus identifies himself as the door. He is the only true and safe way into the spiritual realm. Any attempt to enter by another route—accessing spiritual experiences or power apart from Christ—is a counterfeit path. And Jesus warns that those who come that way are aligned with thieves and robbers—the same evil spirits who "come to steal, kill, and destroy" (**John 10:10**).

God created us to interact with the spiritual realm, but it must always be done through the doorway of Christ. *Any* spiritual practice that seeks access, guidance, power, or connection apart from Him—no matter what name it goes by—falls under the category of the occult. Some practices look harmless, even helpful, but when they bypass Christ they can quietly open doors to torment. This is why two people may appear to be doing the same kind of spiritual practice, yet one is acting through Christ while another is engaging the spiritual realm apart from Him. The difference is not the vocabulary—it is the doorway.

Most of the items in the list below are clearly occult in nature, while others may depend on whether they involved seeking spiritual access apart from Christ. If something doesn't seem to match your experience, simply ask God whether that activity was a form of spiritual access outside of Christ. If He confirms that it was, include it in your repentance list. You do not need to analyze or debate this—simply ask and list what comes to mind. And remember this simple principle: *when in doubt, repent*. If the practice was never a sin, repentance costs nothing. But if it opened a door, repentance may be the very thing that closes it and sets you free.

As you review the list below, don't rush and don't panic. You are not being asked to search for problems—only to recognize what applies to you. The following is a sample list to help you identify those areas.

• **Spirit contact**—Ouija boards, séances, mediums, spirit guides, ancestor worship; • **Divination practices**—palm reading, tarot cards, psychic readings, astrology, horoscopes, numerology, roots or tea leaves, pendulums or dowsing rods, water divining, Akashic records readings, other forms of divination or fortune-telling, or seeking unknown knowledge or guidance from the Universe, the collective consciousness, or similar spiritual sources; • **Witchcraft related**—witchcraft, Wicca/white magic, Santería; • **Healing and manifestation practices**—crystals for healing or energy work, certain types of new age healing, burning sage, vision boards (used with manifestation or "law of attraction" intent), psychedelic or consciousness-altering substances; • **Objects**—dream catchers, spirit dolls or statues, evil eye charms or amulets for protection; • **Spiritual manipulation or superstition**—levitation, hypnosis, superstition; • **Physical practices**—yoga*, martial arts with religious or spiritual teaching; • **Occult-themed games and media**—any occult-based games (such as Dungeons and Dragons, Magic: The Gathering, Pokémon), or entertainment that glorifies dark supernatural powers or witchcraft (such as books, comic books, movies, and series like Harry Potter and others); • **Satanic influence**—singing along to or participating in music that praises or honors Satan. All of these can be open doors to spiritual torment.

** There are mysteries in the spiritual realm that can open doorways into the occult realm and should be avoided. The danger with yoga is certain positions and meditations can open wrong doors and create legal rights against you.*

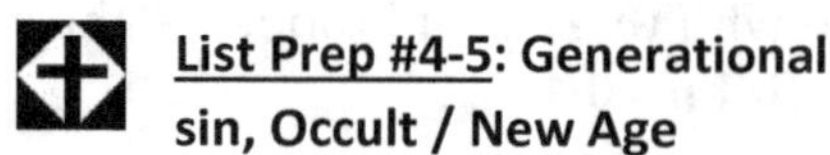

List Prep #4-5: Generational sin, Occult / New Age

Action Item: make a list of **(1)** every type of occult activity you have participated in, *even* if you only did it one time for just a minute or two, **(2)** the *first* person who introduced you to each activity, and **(3)** every subsequent person who encouraged you to do the activity (if you don't remember their names, identify with a description such as "guy in the blue hat"). If you're unsure whether something applies, write it down and move on. You can sort clarity later.

#6 Word Curses

Word curses are statements spoken over you that haunt you, such as "you'll never succeed," "you'll always be an addict," or "you'll never have a fulfilling relationship." These statements have either come true or you fear will come true. They can be spoken about you by others or even by yourself. Once you *believe* a word curse, you give agreement to it. And that gives a tormenting spirit the legal right to fulfill that agreement. This is *not* about reviewing every careless word ever spoken. It's about identifying statements that stuck, shaped how you see yourself, or continue to echo in your mind.

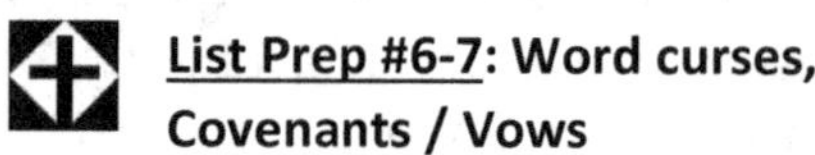

List Prep #6-7: Word curses, Covenants / Vows

Action Item: make a list of **(1)** every word curse spoken over you and **(2)** who spoke them to you (include those you have spoken over yourself). Focus on the words that carried weight or influence—not passing comments that had no lasting effect.

#7 Covenants and Vows

Covenants and vows are solemn commitments you make to others. If you break a covenant or vow, it may allow a spirit of torment into your life. This refers to serious commitments that carried weight and intention—not everyday promises or good intentions that fell short.

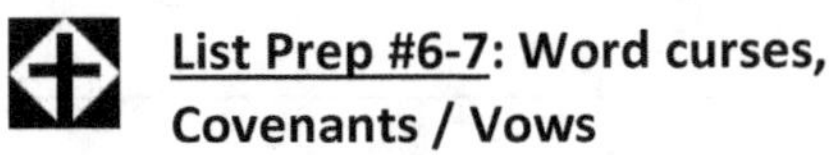

Action Item: list **(1)** all covenants/vows you have broken (ex: bankruptcy, divorce, vows to God, disability (claiming you are disabled when you aren't), etc) and **(2)** any person who may have encouraged you to break them. You are not being asked to judge yourself—only to name agreements that were knowingly entered into and later violated.

____

____

____

#8 Idolatry

Idolatry generally shows up in two ways. One is giving spiritual devotion, honor, prayer, or offerings to gods or spiritual beings other than the one true God—sometimes openly, and sometimes through practices that blend faith with other spiritual systems. The other is allowing something in life to take God's place as your highest priority, source of identity, or sense of security.

In some cultures or family traditions, people may honor or pray to spiritual figures that appear Christ-focused or Christ-oriented in name, but are actually tied to other belief systems or spiritual practices. When devotion, prayer, or offerings are directed toward anything that is not truly of God—even if it feels familiar, sincere, or culturally accepted—it can quietly open spiritual doors.

Idolatry can also take a more everyday form, such as when success, relationships, possessions, children, work, or personal ambition consistently take precedence over God in your heart and decisions. In both cases, the issue is not the object itself, but what is being given ultimate trust, allegiance, or spiritual attention.

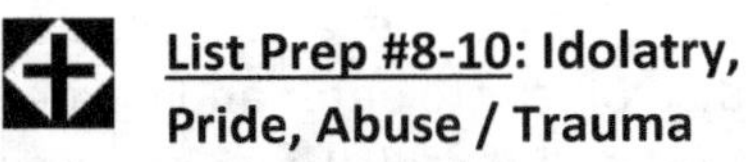

Action Item: make a list of **(1)** all possible forms of idolatry you may have committed *at any time* in your life (even early childhood) and **(2)** anyone who may have encouraged you to do what you did, especially the *first* time you did it. Focus on patterns or priorities that displaced God—not isolated moments of distraction. Ask God to reveal what, if any, actions you have done in the past that may be considered idolatry.

____

____

____

#9 Pride

Pride is the feeling of superiority and haughtiness when you believe yourself to be better than others in a particular characteristic or area of expertise. It often shows up quietly, through comparison, self-reliance, or the belief that you don't need help or correction. This is not about recognizing skills, gifts, or accomplishments. It's about where self-importance, independence from God, or comparison with others has taken root.

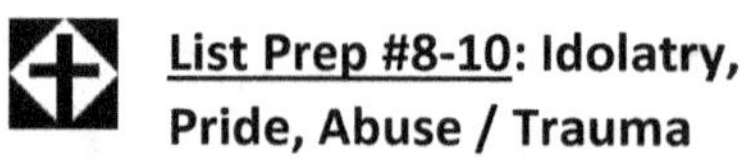

Action Item: make a list of all things for which you are prideful (ex: if you feel you have a better marriage than others, a better ministry, a better profession, good looks). Focus on areas where pride shaped your attitude, decisions, or treatment of others—not moments of healthy confidence.

____

____

____

#10 Abuse and Trauma

Experiencing abuse, rape, abortion, a car accident, or any other traumatic event can potentially create open doors for tormenting spirits. Abuse, for instance, can lead to emotional wounds (unforgiveness) and unholy soul ties with the abuser. Abortion can create grief and generate unholy soul ties with the aborted baby, the abortion doctor, and those who influenced you to abort your child. Witnessing a car accident or traumatic event can instill intense fear, allowing a spirit of fear to enter and perpetuate ongoing fearfulness and even PTSD. This section is **not** about revisiting or processing trauma—it is about identifying events that may have opened doors. You do not need to describe details, emotions, or experiences beyond what is necessary to identify the event.

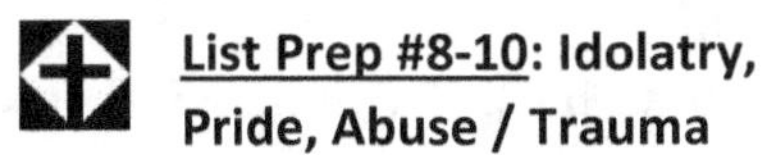

<u>List Prep #8-10</u>: Idolatry, Pride, Abuse / Trauma

Action Item: make a list of **(1)** all abuse and traumatic events (either personal or observed), **(2)** any sinful emotions or responses that occurred because of each event, and **(3)** each person directly involved (if applicable) with those events. Keep entries brief and factual. If an event feels too heavy to linger on, simply note it and move on.

<u>#11 Addictions</u>

Addictions—such as drugs, alcohol, smoking pornography, and sex—are sins that can open doors for unholy spirits to intensify and increase that same behavior. Often, spirits of addiction originally enter through unholy soul ties between you and the *first* person who introduced you to that activity. For example, if you have a drug addiction, there may be an unholy soul tie with the first person who got you to taking drugs (even prescription drugs such as for ADHD). Often, it's prescription drugs early in life that may eventually lead towards doing illegal drugs (this could be a first grade teacher who suggested you had ADHD, the physician who prescribed ADHD medication, and your mother who forced you to take the medication). Or it could be a friend who encouraged you to try a certain drug, and you got addicted. If you have a smoking addiction, it may be the first person who taught you to smoke and gave you your first pack of cigarettes. In other words, *all* people involved with your *initial* exposure that ultimately led to an addiction are crucial to include in this list. This section is not about recounting your entire history with an addiction. It is about identifying how it began and who was involved at key points.

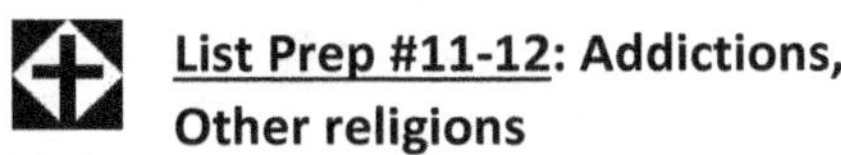

<u>List Prep #11-12</u>: Addictions, Other religions

Action Item: make a list of: **(1)** all addictions, **(2)** for each one, the *first* time you engaged in it and the person who persuaded, invited, or influenced you toward it, **(3)** anyone you have ever bought supplies from (ex. who you got drugs from), and **(4)** anyone you have done those addictions with (ex. who you partied with). **If your history is long**, list the people that stand out or come to mind first. You do *not* need to capture every instance or every name for this to be effective. If you have suffered with addictions for a long time, your list may be extensive. If you do not recall specific names, describe the individuals (ex. "guy with the blue hat). If you sense there are people you're missing, ask God to remind you of anyone necessary to remove the legal rights involved—then continue forward.

____

____

____

#12 Other Religions

(*Note: this is similar to #8 Idolatry but is included here to capture anything not included in that section, especially generational activity.*) Engaging in worship or acts of honoring, praying to, or participating in religious practices directed toward gods or spiritual systems outside of God can create open doors for torment. Worship means engaging in any spiritual act—whether intentional or cultural—that involves honoring or participating in another religious system, even if it felt small or routine at the time. This could include placing food on an altar as part of childhood tradition, participating to honor family customs, or engaging in religious rituals while visiting another country. This is not about curiosity or learning, but about any participation that involved spiritual agreement or honoring.

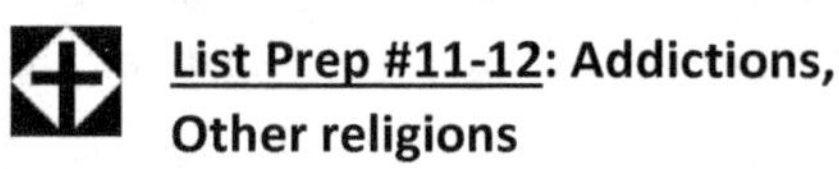

Action Item: make a list of any religions you, your parents, or your ancestors have participated in—through worship, ritual, prayer, or offerings—regardless of how minor or insignificant it may seem now. List the **(1)** person (you or an ancestor), **(2)** religion, and **(3)** any spirit names, if known. If something comes to mind that seems uncertain, write it down and move on. If it was nothing, repentance causes no harm. If it mattered, repentance may close a door.

____

____

____

#13 Judgments

A judgment is a bad or negative thought you speak against someone else. All judgments are sins and, therefore, create legal rights for tormenting spirits. For example, if you tell a friend, "Stay away from John; he's an idiot," that would be a judgment. Judgments are often tied to people who have hurt you in some way, whether you have forgiven them or not. This is not about noticing behavior or setting boundaries. It is about condemning conclusions you formed or spoke about someone's character, worth, or future.

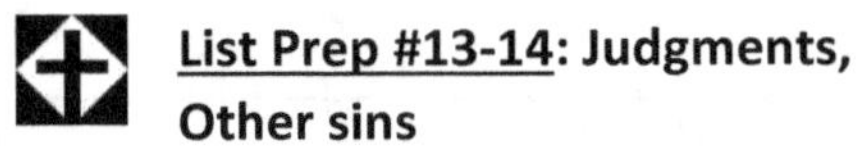

Action Item: list of all people you've had bad thoughts towards and have possibly spoken out against them. Focus on judgments that carried weight, were repeated, or became part of how you saw that person—not fleeting thoughts you dismissed.

____

____

____

____

#14 Other Sins

"Other sins" are any other sins God brings to mind that do not fit into the previous categories. For instance, if you had a health issue where you felt God directing you against a **certain treatment** but you did that treatment anyway, that would be considered a sin. Or, since your body is the temple of God, if you consistently eat **unhealthy foods** or participate in **unhealthy activities**, these may be sin. Or, if you have had an **abortion**, performed an abortion, or encouraged someone to get an abortion, that, too, is sin. Or, if **resentment towards God** has crept into your heart due to certain issues in your life, that would also be a sin. Or, in rare cases, certain **prescription medications** can produce hallucinogenic or reality-altering side effects, similar to the altered states associated with psychedelic substances. In those situations, this can unintentionally open a spiritual door. This is not a condemnation for taking any medication. But if you began a medication and noticed increased torment or a loss of clarity starting around the same time, there may be a connection. This is not something to search for, assume, or fear. This section is not meant to lead to exhaustive self-analysis, but simply to include anything specific God brings to mind that hasn't already been covered.

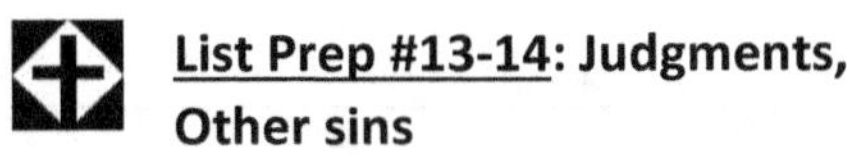

Action Item: make a list of any additional sins you have not placed on a list yet, including anything God reveals you may be doing to your body that is not healthy, entertainment you engage in God prompts you to stop (books, music, movies), dishonoring your father or mother in any way (Ten Commandments #5), or anything else you've done that he brings to mind. If nothing comes to mind, you can leave this list blank and move forward.

____

____

____

____

#15 Agreement Sins

(Note: this is similar to #4 Generational Sins but is included here to capture certain types of sins that require a special process to break) For purposes of this section, an "agreement sin" refers to you or an ancestor agreeing to oaths, rituals, or any other type of agreement that is contrary to God. This often occurs both with groups that use secret oaths (such as Shriners, Freemasons, Eastern Star, and even the Mormon Church's "penalty" oath prior to 1990), and with occult practices such as witchcraft, Wicca, any form of divination (palm reading, use of water or mineral divining rods, etc), or Luciferian organizations. Any occult activity you or an ancestor have participated in (see list in "List #5 Occult" description above) is usually tied to an agreement sin. This section is not about guessing or uncovering hidden history. It focuses on known or suspected agreements that carried spiritual weight.

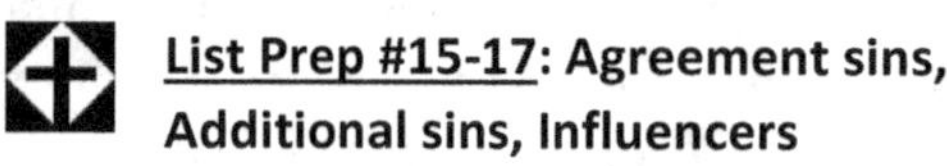

List Prep #15-17: Agreement sins,
Additional sins, Influencers

Action Item: make a list of **(1)** any secret oath groups you, a parent, or any ancestor may have participated in; list the person and the group if known; **(2)** any occult activity either you, or an ancestor, have participated in, *even* if you have already listed it in another list; list the person and the occult practice if known; and **(3)** any other type of agreement or iniquity sins you are aware of from your family line (*even* if you have already listed it in another list (slavery, murder [including abortion], adultery, etc.). If details are unclear, write what you know and move on. You don't have to prove or verify anything for this process to work.

____

____

____

#16 Additional Sins and Issues

While many people have committed some of the sins listed below at one point in their life, the purpose of this list is to identify sins or issues that are **consistently present** in your life. Anytime a sin or issue is *consistently* present, it may be an indication that an unholy spirit is involved. This list is not meant to label you or define who you are. It is simply a tool to help identify recurring patterns that may point to spiritual influence.

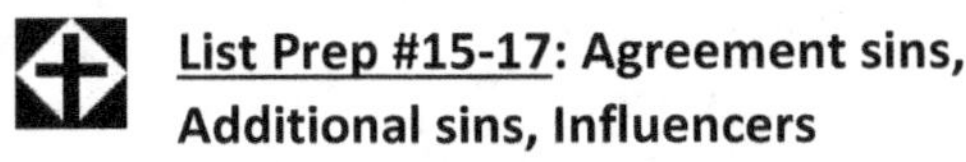

Action Item: mark each item below that you struggle with as a **strong, recurring urge** whenever it appears. Do not analyze, explain, or rank these items. Simply mark what applies and move on. *(The following list is © Above and Beyond Christian Counseling, a deliverance ministry. Visit them at AandBCounseling.com).*

HAUGHTY

Pride / Vanity
Perfection
Accusation / Scorn
Judgmental
/ Condemning
Self-Judgmental
/ Self-Condemning
Competition
Mockery
Stubbornness
Selfishness
Gossip
Boastful
Self-righteousness
/ Embarrassment
/ Humiliation
Sarcasm
Critical

DEAF & DUMB

Mental Illness
/ Insanity
Double Mindedness
Seizures / Epilepsy
Mind binding
Stupor

SLUMBER

Isolation / Anti-social
Sleepiness / Laziness
Forgetfulness
Stupidity
Daydreaming
/ Trances
Apathy / Indifference
Confusion

HEAVINESS

Misery / Dread
Rejection
/ Self-rejection
Despair
/ Hopelessness
Grief
Fatigue / Weariness
Guilt / Shame
Self-pity
Loneliness
Depression
/ Manic Depression
Suicide / Death

FEAR

Insecurity
/ Inadequacy
/ Inferiority
Timidity
Worry / Anxiety
Fear of Death
Cowardice / Cowering
Hiding / Escaping
Fear of Authority
/ Speaking

Fear of Being Abused
Terror / Torment
Nightmares
Panic Attacks
Phobias (___________)
Nervousness
/ Hyperactivity
Unrest
Abandonment
Fear of Future
/ Failure
Little girl / boy
personality spirits

JEALOUSY

Impatience
/ Frustration
Bitterness / Negativity / Blaming
Strife / Division
/ Conflict
Envy / Covetousness
Control / Manipulation
Revenge / Retaliation
Suspicion
Anger / Rage
Hatred / Self-hatred
Cruelty
Murder / Violence
Murmuring
/ Complaining
Profanity

LYING

Exaggeration / Drama
Hypocrisy Religious
/ Legalism
/ Tradition
Word Twisting
Theft

ANTI-CHRIST

Doubt & Unbelief
Rebellion
Humanism
/ Intellectualism
Self-help
Self-exaltation

WHOREDOM

Worldliness
Idolatry
Fornication
Adultery

PERVERSION

Lust
Homosexuality
/ Lesbianism
Gender Dysphoria
Prostitution
/ Masturbation
Sodomy
Bestiality
Molestation / Incest
Exhibitionism
Pornography
Seducing Spirit
Fantasy Spirits
Incubus / Succubus
Sensual Thoughts
Other____________

POVERTY

BONDAGE

Hindering
/ Distraction
/ Greed / Hoarding
Gluttony
Slavery / Emotional Weakness
Addiction (_______________)
Other (_______________)

#17 Influencers

An influencer is the person who *first* influenced you to commit a specific sin. From a freedom standpoint, identifying the first person who influenced you to commit that sin is usually the key to being set free because the tormenting spirit's legal right is usually an unholy soul tie with that person. This is not about assigning blame or reliving past relationships. It is about identifying the point of entry.

List Prep #15-17: Agreement sins, Additional sins, Influencers

Action Item: for each item you marked in List #16 above, list the person or situation connected to the **first time** that issue, behavior, or pattern began. The purpose of this step is not to assign blame or analyze motives, but to identify where spiritual access *first* occurred. For example: **(a)** if you struggle with an addiction, list the person who first introduced you to it or encouraged your initial involvement; **(b)** if you struggle with anger, fear, shame, or emotional instability, list the person or situation that first provoked or shaped that response; **(c)** if you struggle with same-sex attraction or related sexual patterns, list the person or situation connected to the earliest point when those attractions first began to take root—especially if another person was involved through abuse, coercion, encouragement, exposure, or guidance into sexual behavior.

List both **(1)** the **item** from List #16 and **(2)** the ***first* person** who influenced you to do it. If you had been freed from a problem (ex. smoking addiction) that later returned, list the person who influenced you to re-engage in that activity. If the influence occurred in early childhood, was subtle, or the person is unknown, write whatever you remember and move on. Accuracy matters more than detail.

____

____

____

____

____

____

____

____

____

____

____

____

____

#18 Infirmity

Infirmity is any form of sickness, disease, or ailment you suffer with. Infirmities could be things such as: a **family illness** that one of your parents had and now you also have it, **premature death in your family, arthritis, allergies, asthma, cancer, heart disease,** any form of **chronic pain, circulatory/vascular issues, infertility, any type of "disorder," any type of "syndrome," or anything else.** While infirmities are not sins, they may result from sin. The purpose of listing infirmities is to ask God to remove those specific issues from you. This list is not about determining the cause of an infirmity or assigning blame. You are not being asked to decide whether an illness is spiritual, physical, emotional, or a combination. Simply identify what is present.

Action Item: make a list of any infirmities you have and any infirmities you see as patterns in your family line that could eventually come to you or your children. If an issue has been present for a long time or has resisted treatment, include it. You do not need to analyze it—just name it.

____

____

____

____

Prayer of Freedom

Now that you've completed the List Preparation Guide, you're ready to take the final step—praying the Prayer of Freedom.

Approach it with a heart of repentance and faith. True repentance matters—simply reading the words without meaning them will not produce the same result. The power isn't in the wording but in the heart behind it, as it's directed through these prayers.

This prayer is divided into three parts, each with a specific purpose. Here's how they work together...

Prayer #1 repents of Activity Sins, break unholy soul ties, and command all spirits of discipline to leave. You only need to pray this prayer one time.

Prayer #2 renounces Agreement Sins. Pray this three times a day for three days. You may pray them all at once or spread them through morning, midday, and evening. Begin it the same day you finish Prayer #1 and continue for the next three days.

Prayer #3 is a "final cleanup" prayer you'll pray twice a day for thirty days after completing Prayer #2. It reinforces the earlier prayers and asks God to remove all remaining spirits of discipline.

These prayers use the name of **Jesus** because it is most effective, but you may substitute **God** if you prefer. What matters most is your heart of repentance and faith.

If the issue you're praying about flares up and feels worse for a time, don't panic. This is often a sign that you're on the right track and it's actually a spiritual issue you are addressing. If it doesn't fully clear, Chapter 14 shows you what to do next.

Now, you're finally ready to begin the Prayer of Freedom! Just follow the instructions.

For the best results, watch the following tutorial.

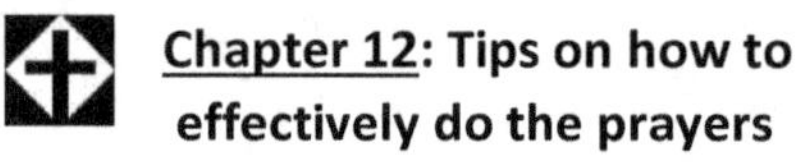

Chapter 12: Tips on how to
effectively do the prayers

Prayer #1
Repent of **Activity Sins**

<u>Pray **one** time. Pray **out loud.**</u>

Lord Jesus, I repent of my sins, and I thank you for dying on the cross for me. I accept your covering of my sins with your blood, and I claim the freedom you have promised from the curse of sin and torment.

I choose to forgive others—everyone who has hurt me, lied to me, or disappointed me, I forgive them. I repent of unforgiveness; I know it is sin. I put it under your blood, Lord Jesus. I repent of anger, bitterness, hatred, rebellion, resentment, revenge, envy, jealousy, strife, lust, witchcraft, idolatry, and all the works of the flesh. I put it all under the blood of Jesus, and by doing so I break Satan's power and legal rights to my life. I repent of the sins in my bloodline that I inherited through my mother and father. I repent of and denounce any contract with Satan that impacts my life that either I or anyone else has made; since he is a liar, no contract is binding. By your blood, Lord Jesus, I free myself from any pact with the devil. I renounce all unholy oaths, vows, pledges, and ceremonies that either I or my ancestors have made. I also renounce and cancel the assignment of every influencing spirit through which I have made unholy soul ties with other people, and I confess as sin, renounce, and break all the unholy soul ties with those people. I also break and release all judgments I have made against others.

I repent of all unrighteous bloodshed in my ancestral line; all sins of divination, whether known or unknown; witchcraft; and other forms of occult activities that I or my ancestors have committed. And by the blood of Jesus, I renounce and break the power of Rejection, Fear, Unforgiveness, Heaviness, Control, Divination, and all other powers over me.

And I repent of the following sins and lay them all under your blood...

1. **Childhood Parent Relationship**

    For father—I forgive my father for (<u>*name each "father" item on **List 1:** Parent Relationship*</u>). Those things wounded me. I forgive him, release all judgments against him, and break all unholy soul ties with him.

    For mother—I forgive my mother for (<u>*name each "mother" item on **List 1:** Parent Relationship*</u>). Those things wounded me. I forgive her, release all judgments against her, and break all unholy soul ties with her.

    For grandparents—I forgive my grandparents for (<u>*name each "grandparent" item and which grandparent did it on **List 1:** Parent Relationship*</u>). Those things wounded me. I forgive them, release all judgments against them, and break all unholy soul ties with them.

2. **Unforgiveness—**I confess that I have resented and not loved certain people who have hurt me, and I have held unforgiveness in my heart towards them. I repent of that unforgiveness. I choose now to forgive, release all judgments towards, and renounce and break all unholy soul ties with the following people: (*name each person on* ***List 2: Unforgiveness***).

3. **Sexual Sin—**I repent of my sexual sins with the following people, break all unholy blood contracts with each one, and renounce and break all unholy soul ties with them, their sexual partners, and those who encouraged me in these activities, including: (*name each person on* ***List 3:*** *Sexual Sin*), and all other sexual partners I may not recall.

4. **Generational Sins—**I confess and acknowledge the iniquities I and my forebearers have committed, and I renounce and repent of those sins and place them under your blood. I do this specifically for the sins of (*name each sin on* ***List 4:*** *Generational Sins*), and in Jesus's name I cancel the assignment of every spirit upon me and my family from all generational sins, and I declare they have no hold over me.

5. **Occult—**I repent of and renounce all activity I have engaged in within the demonic realm and all other occult activities, including: (*name each activity on* ***List 5:*** *Occult*). I renounce and break all unholy soul ties with those with whom I committed these sins, including (*name each person you listed*).

6. **Word Curses—**I repent of believing word curses spoken over me, and I confess they are lies. I renounce and break their power over me, and I renounce and break all unholy soul ties with those who spoke these curses about me, including the following word curses and people (*name each word curse, and who spoke them over you, on* ***List 6:*** *Word Curses*). I also break all unknown curses and those I have spoken over myself. I break the agreement and cancel the assignment of every spirit upon me from these curses, and I declare you have no power over me any longer.

7. **Covenants and Vows—**I repent of breaking certain covenants and vows I have made, including: (*name each broken covenant/vow on* ***List 7:*** *Covenants and Vows*), and I break all unholy soul ties with those who encouraged me to break them, including: (*name each person on your list who encouraged you to break them*).

8. **Idolatry—**I repent of all idolatry, including but not limited to: (*name each item on* ***List 8:*** *Idolatry*). I also break all unholy soul ties with those who encouraged me in this direction, including: (*name each person on your list who encouraged you in this direction*).

9. **Pride**—I repent of my sin of pride, and especially the pride of (*name each item on **List 9:** Pride*). I also repent that I have been prideful about my accomplishments and for not giving you the glory.

10. **Abuse / Trauma**— I have experienced certain abusive and traumatic events, and I repent of my sinful responses to each one, including... (*name each event from **List 10:** Abuse and Trauma—what happened, your sinful emotion or response, and the person involved. For example: "my fearful response when Bill abused me as a child"*). I now renounce and break all unholy blood contracts and unholy soul ties with everyone involved, including all the individuals I just named. And Lord, I ask that you remove the memory of these abuses and traumas—including any from my mother and father—from my mind and body. I rebuke all spirits tied to these abuses and traumas, and command each of you to leave—go now, in Jesus's name!

11. **Addictions**—I repent of my sin in doing the following addictive behaviors. I renounce and break all unholy soul ties with those who encouraged me or with whom I did these activities, including but not limited to: (*name each addiction and individual on **List 11:** Addictions*).

12. **Other religions**—I repent of all idolatry and involvement in all other religions ("including..." *name each religion on **List 12:** Other Religions*).

13. **Judgments**—I also repent of and renounce all judgments I have spoken against all others, including but not limited to: (*name each person on **List 13:** Judgments*).

14. **Other sins**—I also repent of the following sins (*name each sin on **List 14:** Other Sins*).

15. Agreement Sins (**skip**. *this list handled in Prayer #2*)

16. **Additional Sins and Activities**—I repent of and renounce all sins I have committed, and continue to do, that are contrary to you, including: (*name each item marked on **List 16:** Additional Sins and Issues*).

17. **Influencers**—I renounce and break all unholy soul ties with those who influenced me to do those sins, including: (*name each person on **List 17:** Influencers*). I also break all unholy soul ties and renounce all agreements with the *spirits* behind those thoughts and activities.

***Before praying the next section**, you may find it helpful to review the video tutorial at the beginning of this chapter. These steps will guide you:*

1. ***Identify the Strongman spirits***

*Look at "List 16: Additional Sins and Issues." The headings in **ALL CAPS** (such as FEAR, BONDAGE, or HEAVINESS) are the Strongman spirits.*

2. ***Identify the related sins** ("Junior spirits")*

Under each Strongman heading, any sins or behaviors you marked as a strong or recurring issue in your life are the "Junior spirits."

3. Bind the Strongman spirits and their Junior spirits together

*When you pray, name each Strongman spirit in **ALL CAPS** first, then call out and name all Junior spirits you marked underneath them.*

3. Command them to leave

*In your prayer, state that you renounce them, break their power, and command them to leave in Jesus' name. Example: "I bind the Strongman spirits of **FEAR** and **BONDAGE**, and I bind all of your Junior spirits to you as one, including **timidity**, **worry**, **panic attacks**, and **smoking addiction** ..."*

In Jesus's name, I renounce and bind each Strongman spirit in my life, including (*name each Strongman spirit in **ALL CAPS** from **List 16:** Additional Sins and Issues*), and I renounce each of you and bind all your Junior spirits to you as one, and I break the power of each of you, including: (*name each sin or activity marked as an issue in your life*). And now, I declare none of you have any legal right to remain. I command you and all your Junior spirits out right now—get out, go to Jesus, and never return!

In Jesus' name, I bind all unholy spirits, separately and individually, associated with any demonic bondages sent against me or my family, and I break all curses, pacts, spells, seals, hexes, vexes, triggers, trances, vows, demonic blessings, or any other demonic bondages sent against me or my family,. and I command all of you unholy spirits to leave now, in Jesus's name.

Dwelling Cleansing Prayer

Based on the authority I have over my dwelling place—whether a house and land, an apartment, a room, or any temporary lodging—I now exercise that authority in Jesus's name over every aspect of it.

For every sin that has been committed in this place—including any sins of the occult, drunkenness, suicide, bloodshed, fornication, extortion, homosexuality, adultery, witchcraft, divination, rejection, control, fear, violence, drugs, or any other sin—I plead the blood of Jesus over those sins and in Jesus's name I cancel all unholy agreements that have been made herein.

For any unholy spirit that has gained access to this place through any past activity on this property or actions of previous occupants, I revoke that access in Jesus's name and declare void any claim you may have to remain.

If any unholy access points in the spiritual realm have been opened in this place, in Jesus's name I declare them shut and sealed.

I declare this place to be set apart as a dwelling place for the Lord's presence, and in Jesus's name I declare no unholy spirit may enter this place to afflict, oppress, or bring torment to me or my family.

Lord Jesus, I ask that you remove any remaining effects of sin committed here, and fill and surround this place with Your presence and protection.

And now, in Jesus' name, I command every unholy spirit to leave me and my dwelling place immediately. I declare you have no further right to me or this place, and I command you to go *now*, in Jesus' name, and go where Jesus tells you to go.

I also speak to every spirit of infirmity and, in Jesus's name, I command you to go as well, and take all your roots with you and remove all my sickness. ______, go! (*name each infirmity, individually, from **List 18:** Infirmity*—ex: "back pain, go!" Repeat for each).

Lord Jesus, I ask that you enforce my freedom from the curse of sin for which you shed your blood. I ask that you remove all unholy spirits from my life and this place right now. I believe you will, and I thank you for doing so. Amen!

Prayer #2
Renounce **Agreement Sins**

Pray 3 times a day for 3 days. Pray out loud.

(If this feels long, remember: you are not rushing —clarity matters more than speed. And if at any point you feel tired, pause briefly and continue—it will not weaken the results)

(This prayer references your ancestors. You are not praying for them. You are simply acknowledging before God that something may have entered your family line and asking Him to remove anything still affecting you today.)

Since sins of iniquity committed by my forefathers may be imputed to me, and any "agreement sins" made by my forefathers, such as oaths contrary to God, are often binding upon me, I therefore speak to all sins that have entered into my family line, either by me or my forefathers, as my sin. I choose to address them directly, knowing that clarity—not perfection—brings freedom.

Father, I confess and believe in your Son, Jesus, as my Savior, and my loyalties are solely to you and Jesus as my Lord. I now renounce all blessings and all curses of all other religions ("including..." *name each religion on **List 12:** Other Religions*), and of all organizations and lodges, including the Masonic lodge. I no longer want any of their benefits, nor will I be bound by any of their curses. I declare that I am under the blood of Jesus, and the power of these things was defeated by him at the cross.

I repent of and ask your forgiveness, for both me and my ancestors ("including..." *name each person from **List 15:** Agreement Sins, and the group or sin they participated in*), for all participation in any group or activity with oaths, rituals, ceremonies or actions that are contrary to you. You alone are God, and you alone deserve my allegiance. My loyalties and allegiances are to you alone as Lord. If I, or any of my ancestors, have violated the first commandment by swearing allegiance to, or worshipping, a "deity" named Jahbulon* (*pronounced "Jah-bull-on"*) who is not God, or any other unholy spirit, I completely and utterly reject and renounce that worship and allegiance. Additionally, I completely and utterly reject and renounce, whether remembered clearly or not, with the full force of my will, all oaths, allegiances, worship, covenants and participation, either made by me or any of my ancestors, with Jahbulon and all other unholy spirits, including those of other religions either I or my ancestors have participated in ("such as..." *name each religion and/or spirit on **List 12:** Other Religions*). And by the blood of Jesus, your Son, I ask forgiveness for those oaths, allegiances, worship, covenants and participation, both for me and my family.

I hereby break and renounce all unholy oaths and all covenants of any form taken by me and my ancestors, whether known or unknown to me, especially any I may have just listed above. I forever separate myself and my family from Jahbulon and all other unholy "deities" and spirits ("including those of..." *name each religion and spirit on **List***

12: Other Religions). On the authority of Jesus Christ, and not my own, I command you, Jahbulon, and all those other spirits, to release me and each member of my family, and go! I will not serve you, any lodge, or any other religion.

If I, or anyone in my family, possess any objects associated with any unholy organization's oaths or covenants ("and specifically…" *name any object you are aware of*), I break those oaths, covenants, and all legal rights any unholy spirit may claim with those objects. I declare those objects neutralized and ineffective, in Jesus' name. Additionally, I declare all unholy spirits tied to those objects to be severed from them, and I command each spirit to leave now, in Jesus' name, and go directly and immediately to Jesus.

If any other objects in or around my home grant legal rights to any unholy spirit, in Jesus's name I declare those legal rights broken and void and the objects neutralized. I declare all unholy spirits tied to those objects to be severed from them, and I command each spirit to leave now, in Jesus' name, and go directly and immediately to Jesus.

Father, I ask you to block any unholy spirits—those that may have entered my family line through my sins or those of my ancestors—from passing to my subsequent generations. If any unholy spirits entered my bloodline through my sin or those of my ancestors, I ask you to pardon the torment due to those sins and free us from those spirits. Since all of those sins are imputed to me and my family, I repent of those sins personally, and I claim the blood of Jesus, your Son, over them. I also repent for any subsequent sins from those spirits affecting anyone in my family line, even those I may not yet recognize, and I claim your Son's blood over those sins as well.

If any unholy spirits have entered my family line because of a curse, spell, or enchantment done by others, I ask that you give me the grace to forgive those people and release all judgments against them. I choose forgiveness as an act of obedience, not emotion. I forgive them for any effects caused by their sins committed against my family line, and for any damage they may have caused, and I release all judgments against them. I ask you, Lord, to break every curse, spell, or enchantment that is still in place against us.

Father, I repent of any sins that may be the result of generational spirits in my family, and I ask you to block any power those spirits may have gained in my family line because of my own sin. Please heal any damage in my life and in the lives of my family members due to those generational spirits.

I bind, and completely and utterly reject, with the full force of my will, any sin or spiritual defect of mine or any that have been imputed to me, as well as any temptation, allurements, or power that any unholy spirit may have over me as a result of my sin or the sins of any other person. I'm choosing freedom even if it means letting go of what I'm used to.

Father, I ask you to bind, in your Son Jesus' precious blood, any and all curses, pacts, spells, seals, hexes, vexes, triggers, trances, vows, demonic blessings, or any other demonic bondages sent against me or my family or any object we possess. I ask you to bind them all and break them.

And in the name of Jesus and by his blood, I bind all unholy spirits, separately and individually, in my life and the lives of my family ("including..." *name each sin and action, including its header in ALL CAPS, marked on **List 16: Additional Sins and Activities***). I break all curses, pacts, spells, seals, hexes, vexes, triggers, trances, vows, demonic blessings, or any other demonic bondages sent against me, my family, or any object we possess, and I command all of you spirits to leave and never return. Leave now!

(*if you or your ancestors have participated in other religions)*

> I command all spirits of (*name each ***religion**** on **List 12:** Other Religions*), and specifically (*name each ***spirit**** on **List 12:** Other Religions*), to leave me and each of my family members in the name of Jesus Christ. Leave now!

In Jesus's name and by his blood, I break all unholy blood contracts made between me and any other person, whether human or spirit, whether known or unknown.

I also command the spirits of Death, Infirmity, Divination, Rebellion, Lying, Rage, Manipulation, Domination and Control to leave me and each of my family members, in the name of Jesus Christ. Leave now!

I also speak to every spirit of infirmity in me and in each of my family members and, in Jesus's name, I command you to go as well, and take all your roots and sickness with you. _____, go! (*name each infirmity, individually, on **List 18:** Infirmity*—ex: "back pain, go!")

I speak to all other unholy spirits, either in or around me and my family. In the authority of Jesus and by his blood, I break every remaining legal right you claim, and I command you to leave us now. Go, and never return! In Jesus's name, I speak protection over my family. I declare our properties, our persons, and our pursuits off limits to all attacks. I declare every attack of all unholy spirits upon any of us, upon our belongings, our pursuits and occupations, to be ineffective.

Father, I now ask in Jesus' name that you release your healing power into my body and into the bodies of each of my family members. Fully restore everything the thief has stolen, killed, or destroyed. Please heal (*name each infirmity desired to be healed*).

I pray all of this in the Holy Name of Jesus, and through the power of God the Father, and of the Son, and of the Holy Spirit. Amen.

[**Reminder**: Once you have completed the three days of Prayer #2, return to your Issue Grid and rate the intensity level of each item. Also, add any additional items you missed but are noticing changes in.]

**__Jahbulon:__ Per internet research, Jahbulon is listed as "the true name of God" in the manual of a mainstream secret society. It is a composite of three names: Jehovah (__Jah__), Baal (__Bul__), and Osiris (__On__). Baal is an Assyrian deity that led people to human sacrifice, and Osiris is an Egyptian deity. The name Jahbulon is a perversion of the Trinity of God, and is included in certain oaths as the object of a member's loyalty and allegiance.*

Prayer #3
"Final Cleanup"

Pray **twice a day** (morning and evening)
for **30 days**. Pray **out loud.**
(after 30 days, use this as a daily prayer)

If your issues intensify at any point during this process, visit this link:

Chapter 12: If issues intensify during this process

Before beginning, complete the chart below by entering each word curse from "List 6: Word Curses," then writing a scripture statement in the first person (re-writing scripture to claim it as your promise) that counteracts it (ex: if your word curse is *"you'll always be a failure,"* you might choose Jeremiah 29:11 and rewrite it as *"I have been created for welfare and not failure, and God has promised me a future and a hope!"*) (*review the video tutorial at the beginning of this chapter for clarification*)

Word Curse	Counteracting Scripture

Note: Part of this prayer prompts you to repent of any sins you may have committed since the last time you prayed it. You don't need to return to your Lists unless God specifically brings something to mind. This step is simply for anything new He shows you.

Heavenly Father, I come to you in Jesus' name, being made one with him through the new covenant in his blood. I ask for your grace to help me deny myself, die to myself, be fully led by your Spirit, and no longer conform to the patterns of this world. And I commit, and remind myself, to always ask you for guidance in every decision I make that I may stay in the center of your will. Help me to be closer to you, diligently pursue you, and take every thought captive through the Word of Christ.

Please abundantly provide for me and my family—not only in financial provision, but also in health in both body and relationships with each other. Prosper all that we do and grant us the abundant life your Son has promised us.

Watch over and protect my family, and bless all of us to pursue you, to focus on you, to yield to you, to deny ourselves, and bring you glory in all we do. I repent of my sins ("including..." *list specific sins you are aware of*), I forgive each person who has hurt me, and I release all judgments against them ("including..." *list anyone who comes to mind*). And I break all unholy soul ties I have with any person ("including..." *list anyone who comes to mind*). On behalf of (*spouse*), I repent of his/her sins ("including..." *list any specific sins you are aware of*) and break all unholy soul ties he/she may have with any person ("including..." *list anyone who comes to mind*), and on behalf of my children—(*name them*)—I repent for each of their sins ("including..." *list any specific sins you are aware of*) and I break all unholy soul ties they may have with any person as well ("including..." *list anyone who comes to mind*). I claim Jesus' blood over all our sins, and I command all unholy spirits to leave us now! Go, in Jesus' name!

I plead the blood of Jesus over any curse or words working against me or my family from anyone in authority, or who carries authority, or even from my own mouth, for which I repent. I ask that those words be voided, and anything recorded in heaven from them be stricken, removed, and all legal rights revoked.

For each of my family members, I now break, by the authority of Jesus Christ, every curse put upon us. I break all curses, seals, spells, hexes, vexes, and all other demonic bondages, all word curses either spoken over any of us or that have been written or texted, and any other unholy bondages sent against me, my family, or any object we possess. And in the name of Jesus, I command every spirit associated with those curses to be bound, leave, and never return to us.

In the name of Jesus and through his blood, I bind and sever every cord of every unholy spirit over our home. I render every unholy spirit inactive. I declare you are cut off from your communication. I declare confusion into your camp, I declare all your works ineffective against me and my family, and I command you out of my home in Jesus' name.

For both me and each of my family members (*name them*), in the name of Jesus, I renounce and bind every demonic stronghold at work in our lives ("including..." *list any sin strongholds God places on your heart, and include all Strongman spirits marked on **List 16:** Additional Sins and Issues that still remain in your life*). I bind every named and unnamed spirit under each of these stronghold spirits ("including..." *list all junior spirits marked on **List 16:** Additional Sins and Issues that still remain in your life*). I declare each spirit inactive in our lives and I declare all their works ineffective. And now, I speak to each of you spirits: In Jesus's name, I break every legal right you have to remain, and I command you to leave now and never return.

(if you completed the Word Curses grid above)

And Lord, help me renew my mind to believe who *you* say I am in the Bible: (*read each scripture statement from your Word Curses grid*). I receive these truths as identity, not something I'm trying to become.

(if you have had a long-term chronic issue like addiction, pain or any other malady)

And Lord, I repent of my identity of (*name the chronic issue, such as "arthritis pain"*), and in the name of Jesus I command the spirit of (*name the chronic issue*) to leave and never return. I separate who I am from what I have experienced.

Lord, I ask that you enforce the freedom which you have promised from sin and that you remove all unholy spirits from my life right now. I also ask you to release healing into my body and those of my family members. Fully restore all that the thief has stolen.

Lord, I also ask that you remove the memory of all abuses and traumas any of us have experienced—both from my mind and body, and the minds and bodies of each family member. I renounce and rebuke all spirits tied to those abuses and traumas, and I command each of you to leave—go now in Jesus' name!

And Lord, I ask you to strengthen my memory, cognitive ability, thinking power, and imagination. Help me, also, to remember those things I should remember, and not remember those things I should forget.

Please bring forth the fruit of your Spirit each day, in me and each member of my family—love, joy, peace, patience, goodness, kindness, gentleness, faithfulness, and self-control. Grant us mercy in all we do and help us to lean on you each day.

I pray all of this in the Holy Name of Jesus, and through the power of God the Father, and of the Son, and of the Holy Spirit. Amen.

[**Reminder**: once you have completed the thirty days of Prayer #3, return to your Issue Grid and rate the intensity of each item. Also, add any additional items you missed but are noticing changes in.]

Note: for ease of use, we've added Prayer #3 to our app so you can access it any time without the book to help you maintain consistency:

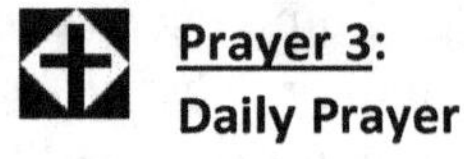

— Chapter 13 — Helping others by "giving it forward"

By the time you reach this point—if you've prayed through the Prayer of Freedom—you may already be sensing something real shifting: pressure easing, old patterns loosening, and freedom beginning to take root.

When that happens, something else often rises naturally alongside it: a quiet desire to help someone else experience the same thing.

Spouses. Children. Friends. Coworkers.

People the Lord has already placed in your life.

If someone comes to mind who is weighed down—spiritual torment, anxiety, addiction, chronic pain, recurring conflict, or a heaviness they can't shake—this may be one of the simplest ways you can love them: **place this message in their hands.**

Not to convince them.

Not to carry the weight of fixing them.

Simply to give them a clear path they can walk at their own pace—with God.

As you read this, if a name or face comes to mind, don't rush past it. Often the Lord brings someone to our awareness because love is being invited to move—not later, but now. An invitation still deserves a response. Notice it—and if you sense His nudge, don't only acknowledge it. Be willing to act on it.

Sharing with family and close relationships

For most people, giving it forward begins close to home.

You already know what they're carrying. You've seen the patterns. You've likely felt the helplessness of wanting to help, but not knowing what to do beyond encouragement and prayer.

Now you have something you can give them: a clear process they can walk through with God.

You don't need to become their counselor.

You don't need the perfect words.

It often sounds as simple as:

"I care about you. I went through this, and God brought real freedom. If you're open, I'd like to give you something that shows the process."

Then you place it in their hands—and release the outcome to God.

And for some people, another simple way to help is to invite them to go through the process with you in a Group Study setting (see Chapter 17), either in person or online, using the videos and workbook that make it easier to walk through the process together.

Sharing in everyday life and the general marketplace

There's a second way this message spreads—through ordinary life.

Opportunities often arrive without warning. Someone mentions what they're dealing with. A conversation opens unexpectedly. A person finally puts words to something they've been carrying for years.

Those moments pass quickly.

That's why being ready matters. Doors like that don't always stay open long—and being ready simply means you can respond while the moment is still there.

Sometimes the door God opens isn't one-on-one, but public. That might look like sharing a short reflection, a testimony, or even a simple mention of what God has done where people already follow you.

Readiness doesn't mean pushing anything. It means being willing to step through a door when God opens it: *"Lord, if You open a door, I'm willing."*

I've also learned to keep a few books nearby—sometimes in my car, sometimes in my office, sometimes in a bag. Not to force anything, but because obedience often has a short window.

Before heading out, I'll often pray something simple:

"Lord, if there's someone You want to help today, make me aware."

Often, that's enough.

Years ago, a book by Bruce Wilkinson made such an impact on me during a difficult season that I couldn't keep it to myself. I began buying them in batches of 50 at a time and, over time, gave away well over a hundred copies to friends, clients, and people I met along the way.

I didn't plan this as strategy—it was a natural response to what God used in my life, and I simply wanted others to experience it, too.

I'm not suggesting you need to do that. But if *The Prayer of Freedom* has brought real freedom into your life and you feel led to help others experience the same, sometimes being ready with a few copies on hand makes it easier to respond when God opens a door.

What to say (keeping it simple)

Many people don't read a book simply because they don't know where to start.

So, when you hand someone this book, you don't need an explanation. One clear sentence is enough:

"Before you go to bed tonight, will you scan the QR code on the front cover and watch the short video?"

That's it.

You're not asking them to understand everything—only to take one small step. God can do far more with a willing step than with a perfect explanation.

That one small "yes," a gentle commitment, often becomes the doorway. Once hope wakes up, people are far more willing to read—and far more willing to pray.

Sometimes this happens in very ordinary settings. You might be talking with a server at a restaurant. They mention something heavy they're dealing with. You hand them the book and simply say, *"This helped me a lot. Before you go to bed tonight, would you scan the code and watch the short video?"*

You don't have to manage what happens next. You've done your part: you placed a doorway in their hands.

Two books, one message

To help people enter this message at different levels, God led me to write two books that work together:

Outrageous Peace and *The Prayer of Freedom*.

They are the same message, offered through two different entry points—because not everyone is ready to start in the same place.

The Prayer of Freedom was the first book God led me to write. And while it has helped thousands experience deep, lasting freedom, I began to notice something over time: only a small portion of people were willing or ready to engage it at the beginning.

Some didn't believe they had anything "wrong." Others weren't ready to consider the spiritual realm, or anything that felt intense, confrontational, or deeply corrective—even though they were hurting.

Then God began leading me to write *Outrageous Peace*. As it unfolded, it became clear what He was doing: this book was designed as the *entryway*.

Think of it like a swimming pool.

***Outrageous Peace* is the zero-entry side**. It eases people in gently—especially those who feel hesitant, guarded, or unsure—introducing spiritual truth in a way that feels grounded and approachable. It meets people where they are—without requiring religious language, spiritual background, or prior understanding—yet still begins restoring peace at the root level.

But it is not just conceptual.

Outrageous Peace includes a simplified prayer process that helps people begin experiencing real relief—often quickly—as spiritual pressure starts to lift. Just as importantly, it introduces them to the One who brings that peace and freedom—God—so they are not just learning about truth, but encountering the One who restores them.

***The Prayer of Freedom* is the deeper end of the pool.** It is designed for those who are weighed down by persistent torment—chronic pain, recurring anxiety, addictions, deep conflict, spiritual oppression—especially when surface-level solutions haven't worked. It is a focused, step-by-step process for going after root-level issues and fully clearing what has been holding someone captive.

In practical terms, *Outrageous Peace* opens the door for almost everyone. And once people begin experiencing real peace, many naturally become open to going deeper. *Outrageous Peace* then introduces them to *The Prayer of Freedom* so they can take that next step if desired.

Both books point to the same reality: **God sets people free.**

The difference is simply how gently someone needs to enter.

If you haven't read *Outrageous Peace* yet, I encourage you to check it out if it holds interest. I think you'll quickly see how powerful it can be—not just for you, but for anyone you want to help.

And because it's only 70 pages and can be read in a single sitting, most people will actually read it. That makes it an especially effective book to give away.

You can learn more at **OutrageousPeace.com**.

Choosing the right starting point

Once you understand the difference, choosing what to share becomes simple.

When to share *Outrageous Peace*

Outrageous Peace is often the best place to start when you don't know someone's full story, spiritual background, or openness. It's short, accessible, and helps people begin experiencing real peace without feeling overwhelmed. For many, it becomes the doorway that awakens hope and opens them to go deeper.

When to share *The Prayer of Freedom*

The Prayer of Freedom is best shared with people you know well—those who are carrying heavier burdens and are open to addressing deeper root issues. Because it goes after those issues directly, it often brings more complete and significant relief for those who are ready.

When in doubt, start with *Outrageous Peace*. It lays the groundwork and naturally points people to *The Prayer of Freedom* if they need deeper help.

Keeping both books on hand allows you to respond with clarity and confidence—matching the right starting point to the person in front of you.

From love to responsibility

At first, most people share this message because of someone they love.

But as you start seeing what God does through these truths, something deeper often grows: a feeling of *responsibility* to help others.

When you know something that can help others get free, you begin to realize it wasn't given to you only for you.

Jesus put it simply: **"Freely you have received; freely you shall give."**

If God is stirring something in your heart—an invitation to step out and help others the way you were helped—the most loving response you can make is to act on it. God often uses simple obedience to open doors we could never force. And very often, that "nudge" is the invitation—God is already making you aware because He intends to move through your willingness.

Someone helped get this message to you. In almost every case, it came through something simple: someone shared it. It may have been through a conversation, a book that was handed to you, a link that was forwarded, or a message you came across at just the right moment—perhaps even something that appeared unexpectedly as you were scrolling or listening.

And if God is nudging you now, *you* may be the person He wants to help **set His people free**. You don't have to be fearless—just willing. And there are few things more exciting than watching God work through you to change someone else's life.

If you feel that nudge, don't ignore it. Respond to it.

If money feels tight

Sometimes the problem isn't a lack of willingness—it's a lack of resources.

If God has brought freedom into your life through this message, you may feel a desire to help others experience the same thing. But frequently, a common question comes up:

Can I afford to help others?

If finances feel stretched, there is something important many people don't realize.

Scripture teaches that caring for God's people is part of real ministry. And often, it begins when He brings a hurting person across your path, giving you an opportunity to help.

If you already set aside money for the Lord's work, then that money is no longer part of your personal budget—it is already dedicated to Him.

Some of it supports your church.

Some supports ministries.

Some helps people in need.

But when God places someone in your path who needs freedom—and you respond to help them—that too is ministry. In fact, helping someone find healing and freedom when God brings them across your path can be one way to live out your tithe to the Lord—because you are using what already belongs to Him to help His people.

Years ago, while I was tithing even when money was tight, God kept bringing people into my path who needed help. I wanted to do more, but I had no money to help them. So, I asked Him if I could use part of what I was already tithing to Him to help those He brought across my path.

I clearly sensed His answer was yes. And that changed everything.

I was no longer giving money I didn't have. I was using *His* money to help His people. Today, **helping those He brings across my path is part of how I live out my tithing to the Lord.**

In the same way, if God is nudging you to set others free, consider asking whether He would have you take part of what you already tithe to Him to keep extra copies of this book on hand to share with people who need it. If He says yes, then you're no longer trying to "afford" something new—sharing this message simply becomes part of your tithing.

And when it doesn't come from your personal budget, I've found it frees you to be even more generous in sharing it with others. Often, one book given at the right moment becomes the doorway to freedom for someone who has quietly lost hope.

Practical logistics

If you decide to keep extra copies on hand so you're ready when God opens a door, discounted bulk options are available at either website so you're not paying full retail.

OutrageousPeace.com

ThePrayerOfFreedom.com

But don't miss the simple point: readiness protects obedience. Moments open and close quickly. If God puts someone in your path, being prepared keeps you from walking away later thinking, *"I wish I had something to give them."*

Before you move on, pause for a moment and notice what's happening inside you. If someone came to mind earlier—or if you sense a quiet desire to actively share this message—that may not be random. Simply ask the Lord, *"Is this You directing me?"* And if you sense that gentle yes, take one small step today.

That step might be as simple as this:

— choose one person

— decide which book is the right starting point

— and make sure you have a copy ready

Love often looks like one small act of obedience—done boldly, done gently, and done at God's direction.

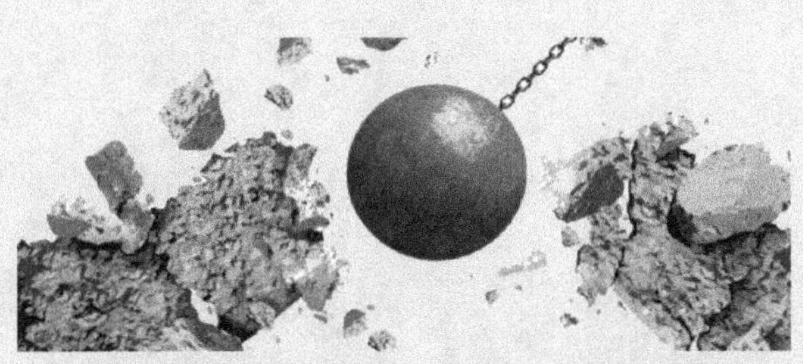

Share your story
Receive a Free Gift

If the Prayer of Freedom has impacted your life, we'd love to hear your story. As a thank-you, you'll receive a **free devotional gift**—selected pages from Beatty's *Nuggets of Faith*, offering deeper insight and practical application of God's truth. Scan the QR code (or enter the URL) for details...

ThePrayerOfFreedom.com/Story

— Chapter 14 —
What to expect after completing the Prayer of Freedom

Now that you've completed the Prayer of Freedom, what should you expect? It might surprise you!

To prepare you for what's to come, I've recorded a short overview with important details I don't cover in the book. Please watch it now...

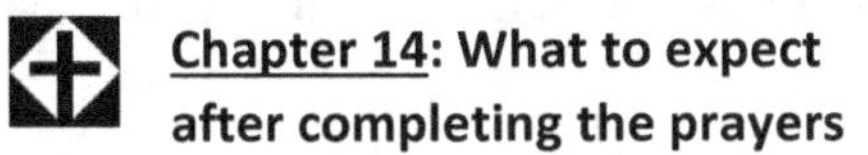

What to do if some of your issues haven't disappeared yet

If you have completed the full set of prayers and some issues still remain, don't be discouraged. This sometimes happens. It usually means a spirit of discipline still has a legal right to you.

This doesn't mean you failed, prayed incorrectly, or did anything wrong. Many people experience significant freedom on their first pass and then discover additional layers God chooses to address next.

If this happens, watch my training below on hidden keys to getting free. In this video I teach how to identify the legal rights you may have missed.

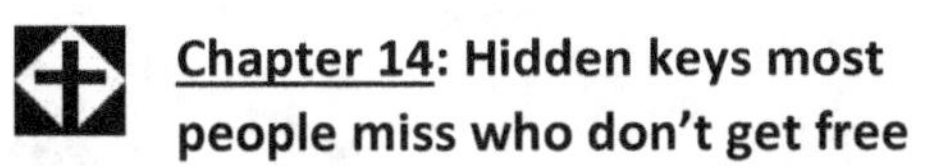

Chapter 14: Hidden keys most
people miss who don't get free

Once you have watched the video above, go back through the List Preparation Guide and ask God to reveal any sins you may have missed *that are tied to the issues you still have.* Pay special attention to "the first time" approach I teach in the video. Then, list any *additional* sins he brings to mind that you haven't already repented of.

If you're going through the process a second time, don't rush this step. This is where my training videos matter **most**—because when issues remain, it's usually because a legal right was missed due to misunderstanding the nuance of a particular category.

And as you do this, be sure to watch the training videos of the categories that apply to you—especially **List #1: Parent-child relationship**. For many, this is where the deepest issues began and understanding it often lays the foundation for true and lasting freedom.

Once you make that list, **(1)** go back and do Prayer #1 for each section where God revealed additional sins, then **(2)** do Prayer #3 twice a day for another thirty days (you can skip Prayer #2).

▸ Unforgiveness could be the key

While on this topic, since unforgiveness is such a BIG issue for many people, it may be the culprit in your situation. Because of that, I want to talk about it here.

If someone greatly hurt you in the past, you may still have unforgiveness towards them even if you think you have forgiven them. If you have unforgiveness, it could be a reason some of your issues haven't disappeared.

How do you know if you still have unforgiveness? You'll know it if your heart is "triggered" by that person. Here's what I mean...

Picture that person walking into your presence right now. What does your heart do? If it is "triggered" and gets upset, you haven't fully forgiven them. If your heart is completely at peace, then you have.

For some people, these triggers don't surface immediately. They may appear later in conversations, memories, dreams, or emotional reactions. If that happens, it simply means God is revealing it in His timing, not that you missed it earlier.

If thinking about that person "triggers" your heart, you must learn to *truly* forgive them to be set free.

Because forgiveness is so critical—and because doing it incompletely can keep legal rights in place—to learn how to truly forgive someone who has deeply hurt you, watch the video before moving forward.

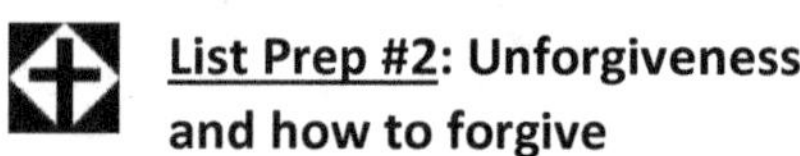

▸ If issues still remain

If your issues still remain after doing the steps above, I recommend seeking help from a trained professional. They can often identify things you have missed and can help set you free. To find someone, ask the Lord to direct you, then search online for Christian deliverance ministries.

Another option is to consider going through my **Master Class** program (see Chapter 17). In it, I go in depth on how the spiritual battle works, how to recognize the key issues in your life that may cause it, and I share many stories and illustrations of identifying hidden legal rights most people miss. Learn more at **ThePrayerOfFreedom.com.**

Most people won't need all of these options. Start with the next clear step God highlights for you, and let the rest unfold as needed.

Another helpful next step is to plug into our *Prayer of Freedom Community*. It gives you a place to stay connected with others walking through this process. You can post questions, learn from others, join live Q&A calls to understand more, join prayer teams, and more. To learn more, go to **ThePrayerOfFreedom.com** and select **Community** from the menu, or scan the QR code below.

When your past has been especially chaotic

If you've lived through years of trauma, addiction, broken relationships, or other deep wounds, it's common for layers of spiritual issues to accumulate over time. When someone like this goes through the Prayer of Freedom, they often experience major breakthrough—but the long history of "buildup" means not everything is fully removed in one pass. It's a bit like taking your first real bath after twenty years of grime. You come out clean, but the water was still dirty and some of it clings to you. One bath helped tremendously, but a second one is needed to finish the job.

For that reason, if your life has been especially dark or chaotic for years, I *strongly* recommend going back through the entire Prayer of Freedom again within the next two months. Start anew with the List Preparation Guide and ask God to reveal anything else you missed or anything that has happened since your first time. And for many people in this situation, going through it a *third* time about six months later brings even deeper freedom. Time and again, those who had the hardest, longest battles tell me that doing the Prayer of Freedom a second and third time made all the difference.

Staying free *personally*

Now that you know how God's discipline works, the easiest way to stay free is to (1) **stop sinning** and (2) **repent quickly** if you do sin.

Let's talk about each of these individually...

▸ 1 - How to stop sinning

There are six steps I recommend to help you stop sinning and stay free.

First (***very*** important), **keep praying Prayer #3 every day**. Make it a regular part of your life. It covers the foundational areas that keep tormenting spirits from returning—especially when you've been set free from chronic issues you've dealt with for years. I've seen many people completely freed from long-term struggles only to have them return after they *stopped* praying this daily.

Sometimes people experience a return of their struggle because they slip back into a similar sin that reopens the very door they had just closed. Prayer #3 helps guard against this by prompting daily repentance. Other times, the issue resurfaces because they've unknowingly held on to an identity shaped by that old struggle. When you've lived with chronic pain, addiction, or any long-term torment, it's easy to keep identifying with it even after you're free. Prayer #3 leads you to repent of those old identity patterns, reject them, and keep the doors closed.

This isn't "maintenance"—it's spiritual protection. I've seen many people lose ground within the first month—not because freedom didn't last, but because they stopped guarding it when they stopped praying Prayer #3. So, if that's you, don't stop. Keep guarding what God has done.

This is why daily guarding matters—not because relapse is inevitable, but because freedom is valuable. What God has done in you is worth protecting.

Second, the most important way to sin less is to spend more time with God. Spend time reading the Bible, praying, and worshipping him on a daily basis. Whatever time you've normally been spending on these things (if any), set a plan to increase it by 50%. Then, once you do, increase it again.

I also encourage you to explore the teaching series in my app, *Get Radical Faith.* Through these lessons, I share how to deepen your walk with God and experience a richer and stronger faith. The more you learn and apply these teachings, the greater your spiritual growth will be.

The more time you spend with the Lord and the more you grow in applying his Word, the more his Spirit will operate through you and the less you will give into sinful temptations.

Third, set boundaries in your life where you know you are weak and are more likely to give into temptation. Satan knows your weaknesses and purposely tries to get you into positions where you are weak. Once you're there, you're more likely to give into temptations to sin. That's his strategy, by the way. If he can get you to sin while you're weak, then you hand over legal rights for spirits of discipline to come in and attack.

To set those boundaries, take the issues you've struggled with—maybe it's pornography, or drinking, or "blowing your top" in anger and yelling at a loved one—and analyze when you typically do those things. You'll start to see patterns as to when those sins occur.

For example, if you struggle with pornography, you may find you often do it late at night when you're tired. Or if you struggle with drinking, it may be after a hard day's work and you want to relax with a drink, or it may be when you're around certain friends. Or if it's "blowing up" in anger, it may be either when certain trigger-words are said, or they are said in a particular manner.

Once you find the patterns when you are most likely to do those sins, simply place boundaries in your life to keep from being in those situations.

Fourth, ask the Lord to direct you on things you need to stop doing that may be influencing you in negative ways and causing you to sin. These could be anything from the friends you hang out with, to the books or movies you consume, to the music you listen to. Everything you allow into your life will influence you in one way or another. And those things that influence you will, ultimately, influence the things you do.

Fifth, get rid of anything you own that could give unholy spirits a legal right to you.

For example, get rid of any **object**, **symbol** or **book** tied to: **(1)** Native American pagan practices (including dream catchers); **(2)** New Age; **(3)** witchcraft; **(4)** good luck charms, crystals and rabbits' feet (anything that promises good luck or power); **(5)** other religions; **(6)** demonic or occult games, or any movies and games with sexual immorality, horror or extreme violence; and **(7)** any letters, gifts or other objects from any ex-relationship, especially if the relationship was toxic and controlling (these can carry legal rights, in a sense).

If you possess any objects tied to a group or organization known for agreement sins or the occult, get rid of those objects as well. It could be any sort of object—clothing, swords, shields, trinkets, coins, or anything similar that may be tied to a secret society, a spirit guide, or any sort of witchcraft, or occult group. Oftentimes, spirits of discipline are tied to those objects and if you hold onto them, you give those spirits legal rights to you.

To get rid of any of these objects, don't simply sell them or give them away because you'll just be passing the legal rights to someone else. And don't just throw them away, either. Let me explain...

I remember a friend of mine and his teenage son were given a painting by a customer of theirs. It was a weird, mystical-looking painting, but they thought nothing of it and received the gift with gratitude. However, almost immediately, the father and son began arguing a lot and started growing apart. Within a few months, they were completely estranged from each other. The son would have nothing to do with him—he wouldn't talk to him, spend time with him, or even acknowledge his existence. It was as if, for some inexplicable reason, the son suddenly hated his father.

Simultaneously during this time, the son went spiraling downward into a deep, dark mental abyss. He started getting involved in all kinds of terrible activities and doing things he knew were horribly wrong, but he couldn't stop himself.

Then, a year later, the father was prompted to burn the painting. And as soon as he did, *everything* lifted from his son and all the mental torment left. The father-son relationship was immediately restored. It was the difference between night and day.

What happened was there was a legal right tied to that painting, and that legal right gave an unholy spirit—a spirit of discipline—the right to attack the owner. As soon as it was burned, the legal rights were removed and the spirit left. However, if the father had simply discarded the painting instead of destroying it, the son's torment would have persisted, as he would still have remained its owner.

This is why it's so important to get rid of *anything* that may allow unholy spirits access to torment you.

And while it may seem a bit extreme, the best thing to do if you have any of those objects is to break them into pieces, burn them in a fire, then scatter the remains far away from you. Doing this has a powerful, spiritual impact in breaking and removing the legal rights connected to those objects.

Sixth, whenever you stay in a hotel or Airbnb, enter a hospital for surgery, spend extended time in any new lodging, or move into a new home, consider praying the *Dwelling Cleansing Prayer* found at the end of Prayer #1. This simple step helps remove any legal rights connected to that space and is an important way many people protect the freedom God has just given them.

▸ 2 - How to repent quickly

In addition to "stop sinning," the second step to staying free is to repent quickly. Here's why this is so important...

If you've developed a "sin habit" in certain areas, it's not uncommon to slip back into those patterns. Breaking habits can be one of the toughest challenges. However, if you do fall back into sin, it's important to repent quickly to prevent yourself from spiraling back into the old habit. To help with this, I recommend using the *3-Step Recovery Prayer*.

Whenever you start to slip back into old sins—like if you used to argue with your spouse frequently, and things were calm until something triggers an outburst and you find yourself spiraling into anger again—this process will help you quickly "recover" and become calm again.

How well does it work?

One day around noon, my friend Luanne called me. She and her husband had been fighting for years, but after doing the Prayer of Freedom a few days earlier, things had calmed down between them. However, earlier that morning something triggered her and she became furious at him. By the time we spoke four hours later, she was still at an "8" on a scale from 0 to 10 and couldn't calm down.

I led her through the 3-Step Recovery Prayer over the phone, and within five minutes she was completely calm, back down to a "0."

This prayer is so effective that I recommend taking a photo of it and saving it on your phone for easy access. Then, whenever you feel yourself slipping back into old patterns, simply use the 3-Step Recovery Prayer immediately and it will set you free.

You can also find the 3-Step Recovery Prayer on our app to access it at any time:

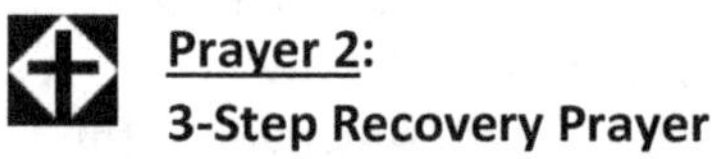

▸ *3-Step Recovery Prayer* ◂

First, rate the intensity of your issue on a scale of 0 to 10 (with 10 being highest). Then, pray out loud as follows:

1. Ask the Lord to reveal your sins:
"Lord Jesus, I repent of my sins, and I ask you to help me recover. Please reveal any sin I need to repent of or person I need to forgive to set me free of (*name the issue you are experiencing*)."

2a. Repent of whatever comes to mind:
(for sin): "I repent of ____ to/with ____ (*name any person your sin was done to or with, if applicable*)."
(for forgiveness): "I forgive ____ for doing ____."

2b. If you mentioned a person's name above:
"And I break all unholy soul ties with and remove all judgments against the people I just named."

3. Command unholy spirits to leave:
"And in Jesus' name, I now command the spirit of (*name the issue*) to leave me, immediately. Go now, in Jesus' name!" (*repeat one more time*)

Finally, re-calibrate the intensity level you are experiencing. If your issue has diminished but has not disappeared, *keep repeating Step 3* until it disappears. If there has been no change, repeat the entire process, asking God to reveal any remaining sin you may still need to repent of.

I also recommend you set a monthly reminder in your calendar to monitor yourself and gauge where you are. If you find yourself starting to slip back into the same problems the Prayer of Freedom has freed you from, it means you've become lax with repentance and allowed spirits of discipline to return.

Many times these things will happen when you engage in sexual activity outside of marriage, or when there are ongoing relationship issues that create unforgiveness and bitterness. Or maybe you had addiction problems before and now feel you are strong enough to "take another drink" (or whatever the urge) and you end up falling back into old habits; things of that sort.

If you catch yourself having slipped far enough that the 3-Step Recovery Prayer doesn't set you free, simply repeat the Prayer of Freedom process again. Make a list of *new* sins you haven't repented of since the last time you did the prayer, then pray through Prayer #1 again.

Expect a spiritual battle after getting free

After you get free—especially from something that had a strong grip on your life for years—it's important to know what usually happens next. The spirit behind that struggle will often try to come back. This is what Jesus teaches in **Matthew 12:43–44** where He says, "When the unclean spirit goes out of a person, it passes through waterless places seeking rest, but finds none. Then it says, 'I will return to my house from which I came.'"

I've watched this play out many times. Someone goes through the Prayer of Freedom, the cravings disappear, the heaviness lifts, their mind becomes clear, and for the first time in a long while they feel genuinely strong.

And because they feel strong, they *assume* the battle is over. **But it's not—for many, it has actually just begun.** This is when the enemy tries hardest to slip back in.

This shows up in real and practical ways. If you've been freed from drugs, it's not uncommon that within a week a total stranger will walk up and offer you drugs for free. People tell me this happens so often that it almost feels planned. If you struggled with alcohol, you'll likely find yourself in a social situation where someone offers you a drink and you take it before even thinking about it.

These things don't happen by accident. The spirits you got rid of are *creating* opportunities to tempt you, hoping you'll give in to them so they can return.

Once a tormenting spirit has been forced out, it cannot simply barge back in. It needs a new legal right. And that legal right usually happens in very ordinary moments. Feeling lonely. Feeling stressed. Being in the wrong place at the wrong time. Having someone say, "Come on, just *one* won't hurt."

If you choose to give in even a *little*, Romans 6 teaches that when you give yourself to sin, you become its slave again. The moment you reach for that drink or take that pill or return to an old habit, the spiritual door opens, and the enemy gains a legal right to return. And as Jesus warns, when it comes back, it does so with a vengeance—"it goes and brings with it seven other spirits more evil than itself... and the last state of that person is worse than the first." (**Matthew 12:45**)

The first ninety days after you've been set free are usually the most challenging. This is when the enemy tries the most persistently to get you to stumble so he can return. This is why it's so important to make up your mind ahead of time that your answer will *always* be "**No!**" Don't test yourself. Don't think you can handle "just one."

And if you ever slip, repent *immediately* and close that door before the spirit gets a stronghold on you. This is why continuing Prayer #3 every day is so crucial.

You really *can* stay free. But the key is you must be diligent to stay alert and resist every attempt the enemy makes to pull you back. If you stand firm long enough, it will eventually stop.

If you want to see how this is applied in real life, watch this powerful short, personal story from Eric:

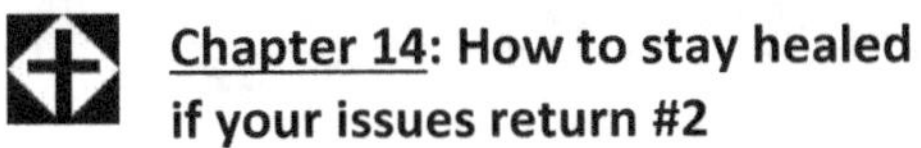

Chapter 14: How to stay healed
if your issues return #2

How to "stay healed" after God heals you

If someone has suffered with a chronic issue for years—maybe some form of nagging pain—and it goes away after praying the Prayer of Freedom, I often see it return to the person. It's as if the spirit of discipline originally causing the pain came back.

If that happens, here's what's typically going on and what you can do to free yourself from it...

As strange as it may sound, when people have had prolonged issues for years that the Lord brings freedom to, they often feel "awkward" without that issue.

For example, "Tim" may have had excruciating hip pain for fifteen years. Now that it's gone, it just doesn't feel "normal" anymore.

What's going on is, over the years, he had become so accustomed to it that he built up an "identity" of being in pain. So, once that pain disappeared, he may have unconsciously thought in his heart, "This doesn't feel right. I should still be in pain." And because that identity is contrary to God's identity for him—which makes it a sin—the spirit of discipline has a legal right to return and keep Tim in pain.

How do you keep this from happening to you? By repenting of holding onto the "identity" of that issue you once had.

You'll see this in Prayer #3 where, if you've dealt with a chronic issue in your life, you repent of any identity you still have with that issue. Thankfully, you don't have to do this forever—just long enough to re-train your identity until you no longer have that issue.

Watch the following video to learn more.

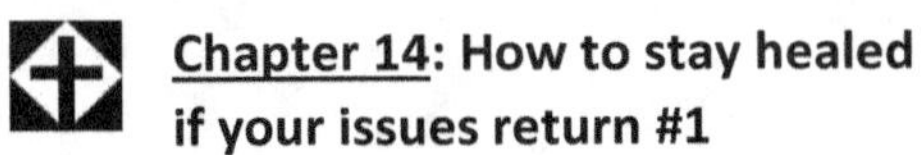

Chapter 14: How to stay healed
if your issues return #1

Continue to grow spiritually

Now that you've gone through this prayer process, understand that freedom is *not* the finish line—it's simply the beginning. As you continue walking with God, your relationship with Him will deepen, your faith will strengthen, and your ability to recognize His voice will grow clearer.

That's why I encourage you to **keep using my app.** You've already used it as a companion throughout this book, but there's much more available.

At the bottom of the app's home screen, tap the **Teaching** tab. That's where you'll get additional training on walking by faith, discerning God's calling for your life, financial stewardship, and growing as a disciple.

The Prayer of Freedom .com

If *The Prayer of Freedom* has helped you, this is a natural next step—an invitation to keep growing.

— Chapter 15 —
Simple ways to help family and friends get freedom, too

Now that you have experienced freedom, start helping family and friends get freedom, too. Here's how...

Helping FAMILY MEMBERS by repenting on their behalf

If the Prayer of Freedom has brought you freedom in multiple areas, it's not uncommon to notice similar struggles in other family members. If that's the case and those family members either can't or won't do the Prayer of Freedom for themselves, God's grace allows you to repent on their behalf.

This doesn't place the burden on you to "fix" them or force an outcome. You are simply bringing their situation before God and trusting Him to work according to His will through this process.

This is all part of another spiritual law we operate in: when we have authority over someone (such as our children, whether biological or adopted), are in covenant with them (like our spouse), or have close relationships with loved ones (such as our parents or siblings), we can repent on their behalf to help set them free.

The ability to repent on behalf of someone else's sins is rooted in "authority." With spiritual authority, you can repent for their sins in relation to freeing them from spirits of discipline. I'm not suggesting that you can repent on someone else's behalf for their salvation, but I've witnessed this authority in action numerous times when it comes to helping a loved one break free from unholy spirits.

If you recall the stories I shared of Dennis, the elderly father who repented on behalf of his adult son who could never recover financially; or the story of Kate, who repented on her husband's behalf when he went into anaphylactic shock; or the story of Richard, who repented on behalf of his son who had gone into a deep depression for years after a terrible divorce—in all of these cases it was their spiritual authority that allowed them to repent on the other person's behalf.

This authority is one of the mysteries of God's spiritual laws. It may not make sense according to human wisdom, but God's Word, along with the real-life examples I've witnessed, clearly shows that these laws allow for it—and God honors it.

It's hard to fully describe this authority and its impact on your family in writing. However, I've created a detailed teaching on this topic, explaining where we see this authority in the Bible and how it works. If you have loved ones who need freedom from challenges, I highly encourage you to watch the teaching below:

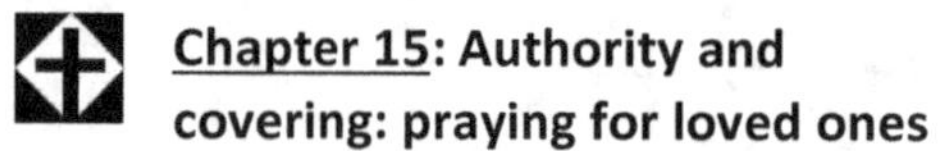

Chapter 15: Authority and
covering: praying for loved ones

▸ How to repent on someone else's behalf

If you want to pray this prayer on someone else's behalf, all you have to do is slightly adjust the Prayer of Freedom process you've gone through for yourself.

First, do the List Preparation Guide again, but do it as if *you* are the person you are praying for. In other words, if you are praying for "Tom," then create the lists as if *you* were Tom. Make a list of *his* sins that you know about. Don't worry if you don't know all the sins he may have committed. Ask the Lord for guidance on what to include, then trust the Lord to reveal what you need to write down. When in doubt, write down whatever comes to mind, even if you don't yet understand why. It may be the Lord revealing something. If you're wrong, it won't hurt to repent of it. If you're right, it might just be the key to set him free.

And remember you are not accusing or judging the person. You are simply responding to what you feel God may be bringing to mind to help set them free.

Second, do the prayers, but re-word them to apply to the person you are praying for. For example, if you are praying for Tom and the prayer says, "I repent of unforgiveness towards the following people," simply pray "I repent *on Tom's behalf* for *his* unforgiveness towards the following people."

Third, if you are praying on behalf of a child (even an adult child), it's best for both mother and father to do the Prayer of Freedom for themselves *first*, **before praying for the child**. There may be agreement sins being passed down to the child from one or both sides that should be renounced before praying for the child. However, if the other parent isn't willing or able to pray, then, when you pray on your child's behalf, be sure to renounce any agreement sins you know of that may be coming down through the other parent's lineage as well.

If you must do it that way, I suggest you also complete the following sections of the List Preparation Guide on behalf of the other parent and repent of these specific sins as you pray for your child: **List 4** Generational Sins, **List 5** Occult, **List 8** Idolatry, **List 12** Other Religions, and **List 15** Agreement Sins.

For a simple, step-by-step training on how to repent on someone else's behalf, watch the following video:

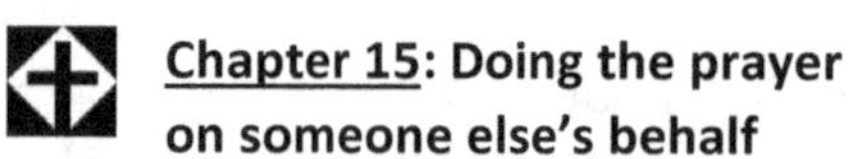

▸ Helping loved ones who can't do the Prayer of Freedom alone

Some people desperately want freedom but can't seem to go through the process on their own. They may struggle with focus issues like ADHD or face intense spiritual oppression that brings confusion, fear, or even physical resistance whenever they try.

If that's your loved one, don't lose hope. You can help. In most cases, this support is temporary. It's meant to clear away enough spiritual interference so they can eventually engage the full process themselves.

There are two ways you can run spiritual interference on their behalf:

First, do the Prayer of Freedom on their behalf as I shared above. This can help remove enough spiritual torment to give them the clarity and strength to engage the process on their own.

If you're considering this, I want to encourage you to listen to Katie's story about her mom. After experiencing the Prayer of Freedom herself, Katie reached out to me, asking how she could do the same for her mother. I encouraged her to do the List Preparation Guide on her mother's behalf, then pray as though presenting her mother's case before God. After doing that, Katie said there was a "radical, supernatural transformation" in her mother's life. In her message, she shares insights into what she did—and offers encouragement how to do the same for your own loved ones:

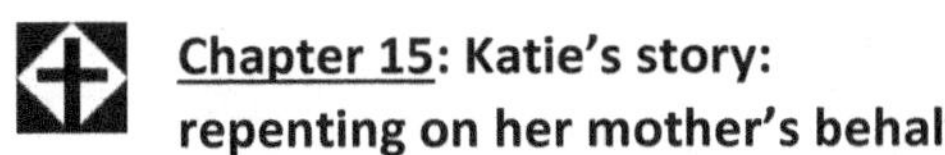

Second, as they begin going through the Prayer of Freedom process on their own, pray the *Beginning Prayer* from the List Preparation Guide (Chapter 12) several times a day on their behalf. This is a powerful intercessory prayer that not only asks the Lord to bring needed issues to mind, but also actively binds enemy spirits from interfering with your loved one as he or she moves through the process.

▸ "Binding prayers" to help children with behavior problems

While "binding prayers" aren't the same as repenting on someone else's behalf, I'm including them here because they can bring temporary freedom for you and others.

For example, if you have young children with behavior problems—maybe they're overly antsy and can't sit still, maybe they've been diagnosed with ADHD, maybe they're always rebellious and angry—sometimes these could be tied to spirits of discipline.

An easy way to determine if it's a spiritual issue or simply a psychological issue is to try a "binding prayer." This is where you verbally command any unholy spirits to stop inciting your child. If you see a noticeable difference in your child when you speak forth the binding prayer, it's an unholy spirit. If nothing changes, try the binding prayer again. Then, if still nothing changes, it's most likely a psychological issue. Think of this as a way to get clarity, not a diagnosis. It's simply a tool to help you understand what might be going on in the moment.

Binding prayers only last for a short duration. Because of that, they are useful for "issues of the moment" but not as a long-term solution. If you want a long-term solution, take your child through a child-level-appropriate Prayer of Freedom, or do it on their behalf.

To learn more about binding prayers and how to engage them, watch my training video below:

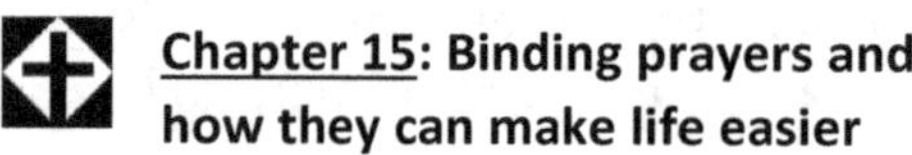

Chapter 15: Binding prayers and
how they can make life easier

Helping FRIENDS by using the Simplified Prayer approach

If you're with a friend who wants freedom from their struggles, here's an easy way to help.

First, open the Simplified Prayer in our mobile app:

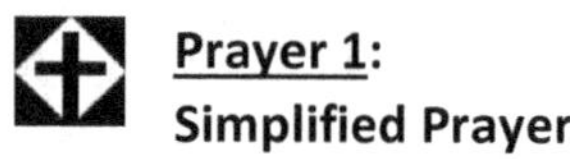

Next, share it with your friend and have them pray through it out loud—encouraging a soft whisper if needed, so they feel free to confess honestly.

Finally, after your friend finishes the prayer, you can pray over them like this: "In Jesus's name, I command every unholy spirit to leave (your friend's name) right now. Go to Jesus and do not return. Spirit of (name your friend's issue), go now, in Jesus's name."

The Simplified Prayer is a variation of what I refer to as the "ad-hoc prayer process." By identifying the key issues in someone's life, you can easily guide them through a simple prayer of repentance without needing the Simplified Prayer in front of you.

If you'd like a ready-made way to bring friends or family together, the **Group Study** (see Chapter 17) is a simple, video-based series that makes it easy to host others in your home, church, workplace, or online and walk through this process together. For many, this can be easier and more effective than simply giving them the book, because they're able to go through the process in a group setting with others.

And if you want to go deeper so you can help loved ones more effectively, the **Master Class** (also in Chapter 17) will give you advanced training, real-life examples, and practical tools to recognize and remove roadblocks when freedom seems hard to reach.

To learn more about guiding friends through the process, watch my short training on this method:

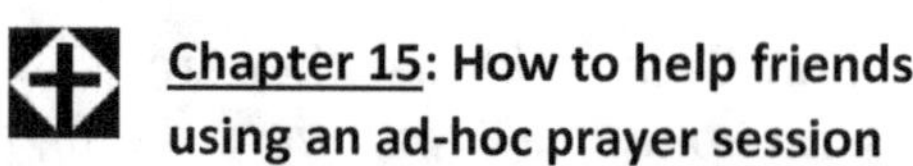

Chapter 15: How to help friends
using an ad-hoc prayer session

— Chapter 16 — Your *next* step: help set your nation free

Now that you understand the *power* of repentance, I want to invite you to participate in the REAL reason I wrote this book.

Besides the Lord directing me to write it, there are two personal reasons I wrote this book. The *second* one will surprise you!

The first reason I wrote this book is to set people free. I've seen so much heartache and so many problems literally melt away in people's lives after they repent that I must tell the world about it! I want people set free so they can pursue their God-given destiny with zeal. I want to see them further God's kingdom here on earth and fulfill the destiny he has for their lives—the "good works he prepared beforehand" that Paul talks about in **Ephesians 2:10**.

So, if you've found this book helpful, please help set others free by sharing it with them. Keep a few books on hand and "give it forward" when the Lord places someone in your path who needs help.

The second reason, the one I want to invite you to help with, is a **bold, *audacious* goal**...

I want to see God heal *nations* and set them free, and together I believe we can do it.

God doesn't heal nations through a few powerful people—but when the hearts of his people turn back to him in repentance.

So, **how do you heal a nation?** The same as you heal a person—by repenting to cast out the darkness and allowing God's light to come in. A nation is only as dark as its people. If the people are full of light, so is the nation.

Imagine what would happen in *your* nation if everyone repented of their sins? If they did, the darkness would leave and the nation would be healed.

For centuries, Godly men and women have struggled with how to get people to repent so they and their nations can be healed. I believe the Prayer of Freedom solves this problem by teaching people *why* to repent. And now, we can finally set nations free!

I live in the United States of America where we face many challenges. I believe the root cause of most of them are the sins we, as a nation, have been committing for generations. And if you live in another nation, I'm certain you can say the same about yours, too.

The Lord called me in late 2020 to repent daily on behalf of my nation. I asked him, "What do I repent for?" He directed me to the Ten Commandments. The Ten

Commandments are God's standard of holiness—that's why they are so holy. Ultimately, most sins are either a transgression against or perversion of one of these Ten Commandments.

The bottom line is, God brings judgment against nations because of the sins of its people. And he relents of that judgment if the people repent.

The book of Jonah talks about a wicked city named Nineveh that had been so sinful for so long that God had decreed destruction against it. God told Jonah to go preach to the Ninevites that, unless they repent, God would bring his wrath against them.

Jonah didn't want to tell them that. Nineveh was one of the archenemies of the Jewish nation. Jonah *wanted* God to destroy them. But God was merciful and wanted to relent. So, ultimately, God got his way and Jonah preached a message of repentance. The city of Nineveh repented, and God relented.

This is another of God's spiritual laws: if you repent, he relents of his discipline... even with nations.

And now that you understand the power of repentance, imagine what would happen if people in your nation began repenting on its behalf, both for their sins and those of their fathers and mothers of past generations. If God spared Nineveh because they repented, and if God would have spared Sodom if he found only a handful of righteous people there (**Genesis 18:28-32**), what would God do in *your* nation if his people would simply repent!

Here's what he promises in **2 Chronicles 7:14 -** "If my people who are called by my name will humble themselves, and pray and seek my face, and turn from their wicked ways, then I will hear from heaven and will forgive their sins and <u>heal their land</u>." (ESV, emphasis added)

There is still time. We can turn nations around!

In **Isaiah 46:12-13**, God is speaking to Jerusalem just "moments" before the city is destroyed, the temple is torn down, and those still alive are sent into exile to Babylon. Times are urgent and in severe crisis. But notice what God says...

"Listen to me, you stubborn people who are so far from doing right. For I am ready to set things right, not in the distant future, <u>but right now</u>! <u>I am ready to save Jerusalem</u> and show my glory to Israel." (NLT, emphasis added)

God is telling them, "There is still time. All is not lost. Repent, and I can save you right now!"

Just as we have spiritual authority to repent on behalf of a child or spouse, that authority also extends to our own nation. You can see Biblical evidence of this in Ezra 9, Nehemiah 9, and Daniel 9. In each of these passages, men repented on behalf of their nation and for the sins their forefathers had committed.

That brings this closer to home. This isn't just something we see in Scripture—it's something we can step into ourselves. So, what do I want you to do? I want you to join me. I want to invite you to **repent on behalf of your nation**... and **invite others to do the same.**

How do you invite others and spread this message? Simply by sharing *The Prayer of Freedom* in the ways God opens for you. Give it to friends or family; tell others what it's done for you; share your story where it naturally fits—whether that's one-on-one or publicly. As people repent of their own sins and see the impact, many will feel moved to repent for their nation as well.

That's how this movement grows—by faithfully sharing the message and leaving the results to God. Start where you are. Take the next step God puts in front of you. When many people take small, faithful steps, God brings about lasting, national change. If we all work together, with God's help we *can* turn nations around!

Below is the prayer the Lord gave me. Please join me in praying it, either daily or as frequently as he directs you. This prayer is about standing in the gap before God, acknowledging your nation's need for mercy, and inviting His light to replace darkness wherever it exists. Afterward, I invite you to pray the intercessory prayer that follows, asking God to set His people free as well.

▸ Repentance prayer on behalf of your nation

Lord, I come to you on behalf of my nation, ____. I bring repentance to you for our sins against you. I repent that we have turned away from you as a nation and sought other gods. I repent that we worship idols our hands have made. I repent that we take your name in vain. I repent that we profane your Sabbaths. I repent that we dishonor our fathers and mothers. I repent that we commit murder, and even sacrifice our own children to Molech through abortion. I repent that we commit adultery. I repent that we steal. I repent that we bear false witness against our neighbor. I repent that we covet what our neighbor has. I repent that we commit sexual immorality, and that we pervert and twist all of your holy standards. And I place these sins under the blood of Jesus. Please, most holy Father, have mercy upon us and our nation. Grant our people the grace of your repentance (*2 Timothy 2:25-26*) that they may repent of their wicked ways and turn towards you, and please relent and withdraw your hand of wrath against our nation. I ask this in Jesus' name. Amen.

Note: spiritual attacks come upon nations because of its people's sins—both activity and agreement sins. The above prayer repents of activity sins. I encourage you to also renounce agreement sins on behalf of your nation. To do this, use the "Nation's Agreement Sins Renunciation Prayer" found in our app:

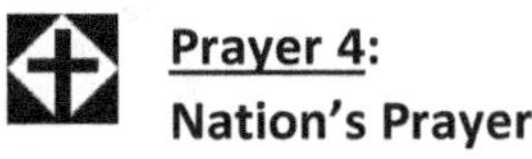

▸ Intercessory prayer to set God's people free

And Lord, I also ask that you set your people free through *The Prayer of Freedom*. Please expand its reach to get it into the hands of your people around the world. As you do, I ask that you open their hearts and minds when they read it, that its message will bring them to repentance so you can set them free, and that they will repent daily on behalf of their own nation so you can set their nation free as well. Please also block every enemy attack that tries to thwart or "cancel" the message, printing, and distribution of *The Prayer of Freedom*. And in the name of Jesus, I bind every enemy spirit set against this message, its printing and distribution, and I declare all your works ineffective. Amen.

— Chapter 17 — Additional ways to grow and lead others

By now, you've experienced the power of *The Prayer of Freedom* to transform lives. You've seen how repentance can break chains of chronic pain, addiction, depression, or relationship conflicts—and how God's spiritual laws often bring immediate freedom when applied.

But freedom is not meant to stop with you. Many people in your circle—family, friends, your church, your community—are still living in bondage, waiting for someone to show them the way out. If you've been set free, you now have a unique opportunity to give it forward and help them experience the *same* breakthrough.

That's why I've created **two simple "next steps"** to help you grow deeper and lead others into freedom:

Step 1: Lead others with a small Group Study

One of the easiest ways to "give it forward" is by hosting a small Group Study. This six-session, video-based program makes it simple to invite friends into your home, gather people at your church, or even lead a workplace group.

You don't need special training or credentials—just a willingness to open your doors and share. The study is designed so **anyone** who has read *The Prayer of Freedom* can facilitate it.

And if you decide to lead a group, you don't have to figure it out on your own. As part of *The Prayer of Freedom Community* (ThePrayerOfFreedom.com/Community), we have leader training and support to help you feel equipped, confident, and prepared. It's not only a place where people help each other complete the process and learn to help others do the same, but you can also safely explore the Group Study before making any commitment to lead. Through live Q&As, training sessions, and support from others, you can learn how the study works, what it involves, and whether it feels like the right fit for you. You can also connect with other leaders, ask questions, and continue growing as you help others walk through the process successfully.

Group studies can be done either in person or online, making it easy to help others experience freedom in whatever setting works best.

Each group study session walks participants through the same truths you've learned, while the videos do the heavy lifting of teaching—so you're not responsible for explaining everything yourself.

This is how lasting change begins—one table, one living room, one small group of people at a time—setting others free from torment and spiritual oppression. Imagine the impact if just a few people in your circle experienced what you've experienced. That's what this study is designed to do.

If you feel led to explore starting a group, scan the QR code below (or visit URL listed underneath it). You'll be taken to a short video where I personally walk you through how the Group Study works, what's involved, and what's required from you—so you can prayerfully decide whether it's the right next step for you.

ThePrayerOfFreedom.com/GroupStudy

Step 2: Go deeper with the Master Class

If you want to help others but don't feel confident that you understand this well enough, this next step may be for you.

While the small group study gives you everything you need to lead others into freedom, some people sense God inviting them to go further—not because they lack the foundation, but because they want greater clarity, confidence, and discernment to help others walk through this process personally.

That's why I created **The Prayer of Freedom Master Class.**

After writing this book, I sensed the Lord prompting me to teach a Master Class and download everything I knew about this topic—from beginning to end—for those who wanted to go deeper. My desire was not only to help people be more successful in getting free if they still had issues after going through this process, but also to help equip those who wanted to use this process more effectively in their own ministry to others.

My goal was simple: to pass on *everything* I've learned over the years about how freedom works. In this training, I go much deeper into the truths and details behind it than I was able to cover in this book. I explain what's happening in the spiritual realm, where we see it in Scripture, the deeper mechanisms behind why this process works, and how to identify and remove hidden legal rights that frequently keep people from finding freedom.

The Master Class includes over thirteen hours of teaching, real-life examples, practical troubleshooting, and recorded question-and-answer sessions where I walk through situations where freedom seemed hard to reach—and show how those barriers were overcome.

This isn't about information for its own sake. It's about giving you the understanding and confidence to walk in complete freedom yourself and help others do the same.

Why go deeper?

For some, reading this book is enough. You apply the Prayer of Freedom, experience God's power, and move forward. But for others, this is just the beginning of a much greater journey.

If you resonate with any of the following, this class is for you:

• **You want deeper understanding** about what's *really* happening in the spiritual realm and how it affects our lives.

• **You want to be better prepared** to use this process as part of your own ministry helping others get free.

• **You've hit obstacles** in your own freedom journey and want practical ways to identify and remove those roadblocks.

• **You want to protect** and maintain your freedom by better understanding these spiritual laws.

A path to mastery

One of the most powerful things about this process is that anyone can do it—it doesn't require special gifting or experience. The Prayer of Freedom is simply about understanding and applying the spiritual laws God has put in place for our freedom. The Master Class is designed to take you from knowing about these principles to **fully mastering them**, giving you confidence to apply them in any situation.

If you've ever wished you could sit down with me personally and ask questions, get clarity, and truly grasp these concepts at a deeper level, this class is the next best thing. Through extensive teaching, real-life examples, and practical guidance, I walk you through everything I've learned, step by step.

Take the next step

If this resonates with you, I encourage you to take the next step. To learn more about the **Master Class**, scan the QR code below (or visit URL listed underneath it).

ThePrayerOfFreedom.com/MasterClass

— Chapter 18 —
About Get Radical Faith Ministries and how to help

If God has used *The Prayer of Freedom* in your life, please help others find it too—whether by sharing the book, the app, or simply telling your story.

Get Radical Faith Ministries exists to help believers grow as true disciples of Jesus. As Luke 6:40 teaches, "when fully trained," we become like our Teacher. Through simple, practical teaching, we help people apply biblical truths that lead to obedience, righteousness, and healing—especially in the areas where they feel stuck, oppressed, or discouraged.

In a time when so many are living in bondage, the need for freedom is urgent. We believe God is using the process in this book to set His people free. If the Lord places it on your heart to help others find this resource, here are a few simple ways to participate:

- **Share our books** with people you love and on social platforms.
- **Introduce this message** to pastors, counselors, or media voices who serve people in need.
- **Connect us with leaders,** organizations, or platforms where this teaching would help.
- **Help reach other languages** if you minister cross-culturally and sense a need for translation.
- **Give financially if God directs**—thank you for helping us keep this message moving forward.

To learn more, connect, explore ways to participate, or to help translate, visit **BeattyCarmichael.com.** Thank you for standing with us as God sets people free!

P.S. If you feel led to give, use the QR code or URL below to go to a secure giving page:

Scan Code now

ThePrayerOfFreedom.com/Give

OUTRAGEOUS PEACE

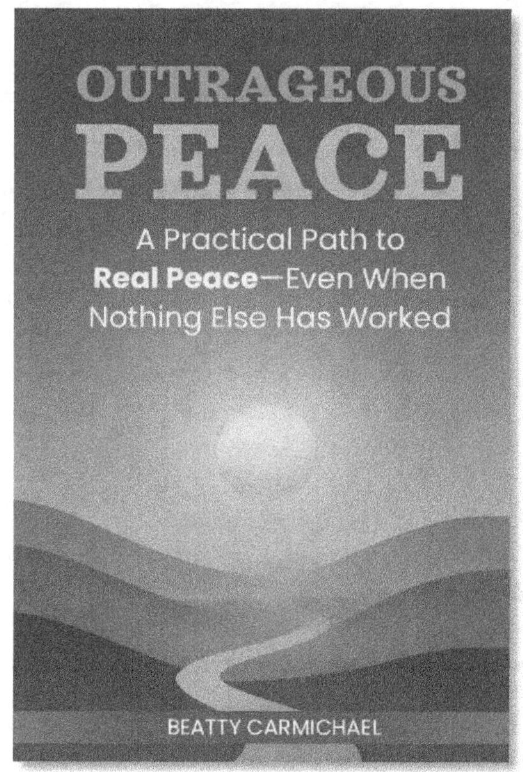

Outrageous Peace introduces the spiritual framework behind freedom in an approachable way for readers who are at the beginning of the journey. Written for those who feel pressure, unrest, or conflict but may not be ready for the intensive process of *The Prayer of Freedom*, it makes sense of what's happening beneath the surface—but without religious language or requiring prior understanding. More than just insight, it includes a simplified prayer that helps peace begin to return as inner resistance lifts. Created as an accessible starting point, *Outrageous Peace* is for anyone who wants peace but needs a gentle, grounded place to begin.

NUGGETS OF FAITH

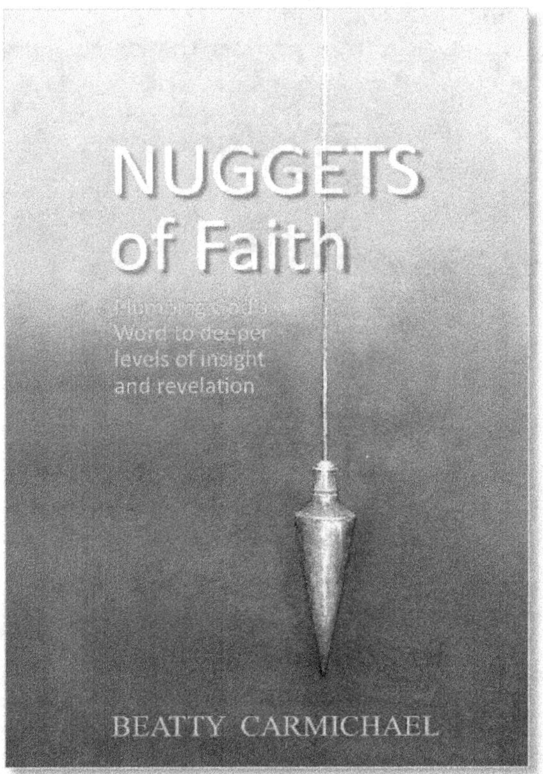

Nuggets of Faith is a devotional collection of insights and revelations God taught Beatty Carmichael over five-and-a-half years of personal study. These entries were first written as personal notes he received from God and later compiled, at God's prompting, into a devotional resource to be shared with others. Written for readers who desire more than surface-level familiarity with Scripture, this book serves as a daily guide for deepening understanding of God's truth and applying it with clarity and confidence.

Other Books by Beatty Carmichael

If you've been impacted by this book and want to explore more of Beatty's teaching, visit: **BeattyCarmichael.com/Books** or scan the QR code below:

Appendix

FOR CHRISTIAN FRIENDS

If you're a Christian, and especially if you know the Bible well, let me set the stage for what I'm trying to do with this message. First, *The Prayer of Freedom* isn't written only for Christians, but also for the wider population. After all, repentance is something anyone can do.

That's why I've written this book to speak to both groups. My aim is for this to come across as a biblical message, not merely a religious one—a message that even those who have rejected the church or organized religion can still recognize as relevant to their lives.

When readers take these truths to heart, they'll discover God's love and the path He's made for their healing and breakthrough. My hope is that this will open the door for them to experience God's love personally and, in time, begin a relationship with Him.

Because this purpose is so important, I also want to explain how I've written this book. The foundation I'm drawing from is a complex theological topic, and I realize some readers—especially my Christian friends—may approach it with deeper theological training than most.

As you read, there are two key things to keep in mind. First, my audience is made up of everyday people, many of whom may have never set foot in a church. Second, my goal is to encourage them to take action with the Prayer of Freedom rather than first exploring its full theological foundation.

Because of this wider audience, you'll notice moments where I use language or metaphors that may sound different from traditional church vocabulary—sometimes drawing from terms common in our culture's spiritual conversations. This is intentional, not compromise. Even in Scripture we see examples—like Philip in Acts—where God's healing opened the door for hearts to receive truth. My aim is similar: to help people experience God's love and freedom so they become open to the One who heals.

A Clarification on Repentance, the Name of God, and Outreach Beyond the Church

Because this question comes up often—especially among sincere, Bible-grounded believers—I want to address it directly.

Some have asked why, when teaching repentance and freedom—either here in this book or on various shows where I'm a guest—I don't always emphasize the specific use of the name of Jesus when speaking to non-Christian audiences, and whether this approach compromises the gospel or its intended end.

It does not.

What the Lord has consistently shown me is that God responds to repentance based on the heart, not the person's level of revelation or the vocabulary they use when they turn toward Him. Throughout Scripture, we see God accept repentance long before the name of Jesus was revealed to humanity. Ahab repented and God responded. Job repented on behalf of his children, and God received it. Nineveh repented, and God relented. None of them invoked the name of Jesus—yet their repentance was accepted because, as Scripture tells us, the Lamb had already been slain before the foundation of the world.

The authority of Jesus' name is unquestionable. However, the Prayer of Freedom is not about invoking authority to overpower spiritual forces. It is about *repentance*—bringing the heart back into alignment with God. When people repent, God responds. And when God responds, torment ends.

When I speak on platforms outside the church—including podcasts, interviews, or shows with a spiritual or alternative focus—I intentionally meet people at the level of revelation they currently have. That often means using language they already understand rather than traditional Christian vocabulary—not as a belief system, but as a bridge. Across cultures and languages, people recognize there is a Creator, even if they do not yet know Him fully or by name. What they call Him in their own language—God, Yahweh, Dios, Allah, or another term—is not what determines whether repentance is genuine. What matters is the posture of the heart.

This is why I do not reject opportunities to share this message simply because the audience or platform is not explicitly Christian. None of us came to Christ with full understanding. We were all drawn, step by step. Repentance opens the door; freedom creates hunger; hunger leads to deeper revelation; and revelation leads people toward Christ.

In practice, I have consistently seen that when sin and spiritual obstruction are removed, people do not drift farther from God—they grow closer to Him. Their relationship with Him deepens, not diminishes. What begins as obedience often becomes love.

So, while this book—and my public interviews—are written and spoken in a way that is accessible beyond the church, they are not offered apart from Christ. It is written in obedience to Him—and with trust that His Spirit is fully capable of continuing the work of revelation once repentance has done its part.

With these priorities in mind, I've embraced two key principles while writing this book...

▸ Simplicity over precision

The first principle is simplicity over precision.

Whenever you simplify a complex subject, you will usually lose precision. And if you've been trained to be theologically precise, you'll see instances where I am less theologically precise than I could be.

However, since my objective is to teach the practical reasons for doing the Prayer of Freedom rather than explaining the theology behind it, I have greatly simplified, and even generalized at times, certain aspects to the point of being theologically imprecise.

It's similar to what Jesus did when teaching his disciples the Parable of the Unmerciful Servant that I discuss in Chapter 4.

In that parable, Jesus teaches the consequences one will receive if he doesn't forgive others. But you could almost say his teaching is theologically *imprecise*. Why? Because it's in the form of a parable, and parables only give shadows of truths, not the full precision of those truths.

But his objective wasn't to be theologically precise; it was only to be precise *enough* to teach his disciples *why* they should forgive (so their heavenly Father wouldn't turn them over to the jailer to be tortured - **Matthew 18:34-35**).

In a similar way, I have simplified certain aspects in this book to such a degree that they, too, are theologically imprecise. They are only precise *enough* to teach readers *why* they should repent (to be set free from their issues).

For example, one term I use is "spirits of discipline." I coined this term to help readers visualize an important truth drawn from **Deuteronomy 28:58-61** and **James 5:16:** sin against God can bring consequences such as sickness, disease, or disaster, but confessing those sins can remove them. In other words, sin opens the door to affliction, while repentance closes it. So, while "spirits of discipline" is not a biblical term and is not theologically precise, I use it as a teaching framework to make a complex idea easier to grasp.

Additionally, the phrase "spirits of discipline" is not intended as a doctrinal statement about the exact mechanism behind what is happening. It is simply a teaching framework I use to describe a pattern I have repeatedly seen while praying with people over many years. In other words, it is an attempt to explain what seems to be happening, not a claim that I fully understand how it works.

Once readers can picture what this represents, it helps direct them toward my ultimate purpose: encouraging them to "confess their sins that they may be healed" (**James 5:16**, paraphrased).

I realize the phrase "spirits of discipline" might raise some questions, so let me explain what I mean by it...

Some may wonder if I'm suggesting that God designed or assigned these spirits to bring affliction. I'm not. I don't believe God creates spirits to be evil, nor that He sends evil spirits to harm people.

But what I *am* saying is this: when we open the door through sin, within the framework I describe in this book, it appears that Satanic spiritual forces can gain what could be described as a legal right to oppress us (**Revelation 12:10** calls Satan "the accuser of the brethren" —he accuses us before God when we sin, and those accusations seem to become the basis for his legal right to oppress us). In this way, their presence in our lives often appears connected to patterns of sin and, in a sense, an assignment from Satan—but not from God.

Yet in His sovereignty, God is able to take even what the enemy intends for harm and use it for good. This is reflected in what Jesus says in **Revelation 3:19**: "Those whom I love, I reprove and discipline; therefore, be zealous and *repent.*" In other words, God's loving discipline is meant to move us toward repentance so the discipline can stop. And since repentance is the very thing that causes our issues to be removed, it suggests that—whatever the mechanism may be—these spiritual afflictions function as a vehicle through which discipline operates.

My goal is not to persuade you to accept my explanation of the mechanism, but to invite you to test whether this process produces the kind of freedom Scripture repeatedly associates with repentance— because **the focus of this book is not on explaining *how* the mechanism works, but on recognizing the principle that when people repent, these kinds of afflictions often disappear.**

▸ Statements over explanations

To keep this book shorter, I also embraced making statements rather than giving explanations when the full explanation isn't crucial to my objective. Most statements I make are supported in Scripture; others are from patterns I have repeatedly observed over the years while praying with people from a wide variety of backgrounds.

If you have questions on the scriptural accuracy of some of these statements, please review my full teaching on this subject where I cover the Biblical references in more detail. You can find this teaching in some of my older Spiritual Warfare teachings found on my website GetRadicalFaith.org, on my mobile app: *Get Radical Faith*, and especially in my Master Class program.

Do Christians Still Need to Repent?

One of the most common questions I hear from believers is this: *If my sins are forgiven because of Jesus' blood, do I really need to repent of my sins?* It's a fair question. After all, Scripture tells us that Christ's sacrifice paid for sin once for all. But if that were the whole story, then why does the Bible keep instructing believers to repent?

The reality is God's Word consistently calls His people—believers—to confess and turn from sin. In **Revelation 2 and 3**, Jesus addresses the churches and repeatedly tells them to repent. In **James 5:16**, we are told to confess our sins so that we may be healed. And in the prayer Jesus Himself taught us, He includes, "forgive us our sins, as we forgive those who have sinned against us." These instructions weren't written to outsiders—they were written to those already in the faith.

So why the emphasis on repentance if forgiveness flows from Christ's finished work? Because repentance isn't about re-earning salvation. It's about restoring fellowship and removing the footholds or strongholds sin creates in our lives. Think of it this way: a child is always part of the family, no matter what. But when that child rebels, the relationship is strained. Repentance is how we humble ourselves, return to our Father, and allow His grace to remove the blockages sin has caused.

In my experience praying with people—both for healing and deliverance—I have seen countless examples where repentance led to freedom. Believers who carried pain, anxiety, depression, or relational strife for years found release the moment they confessed specific sins and turned from them. This was not because Christ's blood was insufficient, but because repentance made room for them to experience the full benefit of what His sacrifice accomplished.

That's why throughout this book you'll see me use "repentance" and "confession" almost interchangeably. Technically, there are distinctions, but for my purposes they both describe the act of agreeing with God about our sin, turning from it, and asking Him to bring freedom. Whether you call it repentance or confession, the heart is the same: we acknowledge our sin before God, and He is faithful to forgive us and cleanse us (**1 John 1:9**).

So, if you've wondered whether Christians still need to repent, the answer is *yes*—not to secure forgiveness again, but to walk in the fullness of freedom He intends.

Repetition in the Prayer of Freedom

Some Christians have also expressed concern about the repetition found in the Prayer of Freedom, believing that repeated prayers are "vain repetition." I want to address that concern directly, because Scripture clearly distinguishes between meaningless repetition and persistent, faith-filled prayer. Jesus did not forbid repetition itself—He warned against repeating empty or mechanical words, as was common in pagan practices. Biblical repetition, by contrast, is an expression of persistence, trust, and expectation that God will respond.

When Jesus taught, "Ask and it will be given to you; seek and you will find; knock and the door will be opened," the original language carries the idea of ongoing action—ask and keep asking, seek and keep seeking, knock and keep knocking. Likewise, in **Luke 18**, Jesus explicitly taught His disciples that they "should always pray and not give up." Persistence in prayer is not unbelief; it is often the clearest expression of faith.

There is also a practical spiritual reason for repetition. The Prayer of Freedom is a process of repentance and spiritual clearing. Scripture consistently presents demonic spirits as real, personal beings without bodies, and they do not simply leave because their legal right has been removed. Even Jesus did not command unclean spirits out only once. In **Mark 5**, the text tells us that He was *saying*, "Come out of the man," indicating Jesus continued commanding multiple times before the spirits finally left. If Jesus Himself persisted, it should not surprise us that we must do the same.

For this reason, the Prayer of Freedom is structured as three prayers prayed repeatedly over time. This repetition is intentional and biblical—not vain, not ritualistic, and not empty. It is continued repentance and sustained command until freedom is fully established. The repetition is not the focus; freedom is.

What if you disagree with my framework?

The Prayer of Freedom is straightforward: repent of the sins God brings to mind, ask him to remove the discipline ("issues") in your life, and he does. The results of this approach have been so consistent that I believe they are strong enough to deserve serious consideration and testing.

As for the mechanics behind why it works, I'll admit I don't fully comprehend all of God's truths. In fact, I'm convinced I understand less than 1% of them—and I imagine you might say the same. Because of that, it's difficult to be overly dogmatic or insist that I've completely "nailed" every theological explanation behind this approach. However, what matters more than fully grasping the reasoning is recognizing that it works. So, as you read, I encourage you to stay focused on that.

Jeremiah 28:9 says (paraphrased), "If a prophet's prediction comes true, it is proof he was sent by the Lord." So, if you end up disagreeing with my simplistic framework for explaining why this approach to prayer may work, don't reject the prayer process itself.

My hope is you will have enough confidence from the stories I share and the surveys I've done to accept the fact that this approach to prayer consistently works. And because it is easy enough to verify, I challenge you to put it to the test and let the Lord prove it true or not.

Since the focus is simply to repent of sin and ask God to remove issues from your life, there are **no negative repercussions** for doing so. If nothing seems to happen, the only thing you will have done is repent of sin—and that always pleases God. In other words, there's no downside and no risk in testing it out.

Finally, if you are a pastor or priest, I hope you'll see enough value in the Prayer of Freedom to test it within your congregation.

Here's a simple way to perform that test. Identify five members struggling with various issues—depression, anxiety, chronic pain, family or health problems, addictions, etc. Have them go through the prayer as I outline in Part 2. Then tabulate their results.

Once you see what God does, I'm sure you'll want to share this with your entire congregation!

Before returning to where you were in the book, if you have *any* concern about the idea that sin can be the cause of sickness or affliction, I encourage you to first read **Chapters 7 and 8.** For many believers, especially those who have been taught that sin no longer carries consequence in the life of a Christian, this can be one of the hardest parts of this message to accept. Yet Scripture repeatedly shows that sin can still bring real consequences—even in the lives of God's people—and that repentance can remove them. In Chapters 7 and 8, I walk through several scriptural examples that make this pattern much clearer. So, if this part of the message creates hesitation for you, start there first. Let those chapters lay the biblical foundation, and then continue reading from where you left off.

ABOUT THE AUTHOR

Beatty Carmichael is a passionate follower of Jesus Christ, gifted Bible teacher, and founder of Get Radical Faith Ministries. His mission is to help people experience true freedom from mental torment, chronic pain, addictions, and other struggles that medicine and counseling often cannot resolve.

For years, Beatty has taught in-depth Bible truths and spiritual principles that bring real-world transformation. Through his step-by-step prayer process, thousands have experienced breakthrough freedom—with nearly 90% success, often in a single day.

As the leader of Get Radical Faith Ministries, Beatty is deeply committed to training others to walk as true disciples of Christ. Guided by **Luke 6:40**—"a disciple is not above the teacher, but when fully trained will become like the teacher"—he focuses on teaching others how to walk in greater righteousness and faith. His ministry provides in-depth biblical teaching and practical applications designed to help others not just know the Word, but live it out in daily victory.

To learn more about his teachings, request a speaking engagement, or partner with the ministry, visit **BeattyCarmichael.com** or download the free **Get Radical Faith** app.

Answer Key

Session 1: Sin and Discipline (part 1) Answer Key

Panorama Overview of this course

- **Session 1:** Sin and Discipline
- **Session 2:** What the Bible says about sin and consequence
- **Session 3:** Legal Rights in the spiritual realm
- **Session 4:** 3 Types of Legal Rights and how to get free
- **Session 5:** Covering and Authority
- **Session 6:** Success Tips and List Preparation Guide

Overview

Sin is a significant cause of sickness, infirmity, and all kinds of life issues

Not all illnesses are tied to sin... ...but many of the issues we deal with *are.*

- It's all part of God's plan to give you abundant life
- **John 10:10** (ESV) - "The thief comes to steal, kill, and destroy, but I came that [you] may have life, and have it abundantly."

Discipline vs Punishment

- Discipline is for correction; punishment is for penalty.
- Discipline restores a person; punishment casts the person away.

God's spiritual laws of discipline

- **Heb 12:4-6 (NIV) -** [4] In your struggle against sin, you have not yet resisted to the point of shedding your blood. [5] And have you completely forgotten this word of encouragement that addresses you as a father addresses his son? It says, "My son, do not make light of the Lord's discipline, and do not lose heart when he rebukes you, [6] because the Lord disciplines the one he loves, and he chastens everyone he accepts as his son."

- If you are his child, God *will* discipline you when you sin... even if you live a "righteous" life

Session 2: Sin and Discipline (part 2) Answer Key

The spiritual realm

- This is where God's discipline occurs

- **Eph 6:12 (ESV) -** For we do not wrestle against flesh and blood, but against the rulers, against the authorities, against the cosmic powers over this present darkness, against the spiritual forces of evil in the heavenly places.
- **TLB version: -** For we are not fighting against people made of flesh and blood, but against persons without bodies...

PERSONS WITHOUT BODIES...

▶ Good spirits

- **Holy Spirit - Gen 1:1-2 (ESV) -** [1] In the beginning, God created the heavens and the earth. [2] The earth was without form and void, and darkness was over the face of the deep. And the Spirit of God was hovering over the face of the waters.
- **Angels** -- spirit beings, and they are also "persons"
- **Spirit of skill - Exo 28:3 (ESV) -** You shall speak to all the skillful, whom I have filled with a spirit of skill, that they make Aaron's garments to consecrate him for my priesthood.
- **Spirit of wisdom - Deu 34:9 (ESV) -** And Joshua the son of Nun was full of the spirit of wisdom, for Moses had laid his hands on him. So the people of Israel obeyed him and did as the LORD had commanded Moses.
- **Spirit of truth - Joh 16:13 (ESV) -** When the Spirit of truth comes, he will guide you into all the truth, for he will not speak on his own authority, but whatever he hears he will speak, and he will declare to you the things that are to come.
- **Spirit of gentleness - 1 Cor 4:21 (ESV) -** What do you wish? Shall I come to you with a rod, or with love in a spirit of gentleness?

▸ Bad spirits

- **Spirit of jealousy - Num 5:14 (ESV) -** and if the spirit of jealousy comes over him and he is jealous of his wife who has defiled herself, or if the spirit of jealousy comes over him and he is jealous of his wife, though she has not defiled herself
- **Spirit of terror - 1 Sam 16:14 (ESV) -** Now the Spirit of the LORD departed from Saul, and a harmful spirit from the LORD tormented him.
- **Spirit of lying - 1 Kings 22:21-22 (ESV) -** [21] Then a spirit came forward and stood before the LORD, saying, 'I will entice him.' [22] And the LORD said to him, 'By what means?' And he said, 'I will go out, and will be a lying spirit in the mouth of all his prophets.' And he said, 'You are to entice him, and you shall succeed; go out and do so.'
- **Spirit of confusion - Isai 19:14 (ESV) -** The LORD has mingled within her a spirit of confusion, and they will make Egypt stagger in all its deeds, as a drunken man staggers in his vomit.
- **Spirit of whoredom - Hos 4:12 (ESV) -** My people inquire of a piece of wood, and their walking staff gives them oracles. For a spirit of whoredom has led them astray, and they have left their God to play the whore.
- **Spirit of divination - Act 16:16 (ESV) -** As we were going to the place of prayer, we were met by a slave girl who had a spirit of divination and brought her owners much gain by fortune-telling.
- **Spirit of fear - 2 Tim 1:7 (NASB) -** For God has not given us a spirit of fear, but of power and of love and of a sound mind.

▸ Additional bad spirits (not referenced in Bible)

- Spirit of addiction
- Spirit of depression
- Spirit of heaviness
- Spirit of anger
- Spirit of violence
- Spirit of pain
- Spirit of suicide

▶ Infirmity spirits

- **Spirit of muteness and seizures - Mar 9:17-18 (ESV) -** [17] And someone from the crowd answered him, "Teacher, I brought my son to you, for he has a spirit that makes him mute. [18] And whenever it seizes him, it throws him down, and he foams and grinds his teeth and becomes rigid. So I asked your disciples to cast it out, and they were not able."
- **Spirit of Fever - Luk 4:38-39 (ESV) -** [38] Jesus left the synagogue and went to the home of Simon. Now Simon's mother-in-law was suffering from a high fever, and they asked Jesus to help her. [39] So he bent over her and rebuked the fever, and it left her. She got up at once and began to wait on them.
- **Spirit of "Bent Spine Syndrome"** (camptocormia) - **Luk 13:10-11 (ESV)** - [10] On a Sabbath Jesus was teaching in one of the synagogues, [11] and a woman was there who had been crippled by a spirit for eighteen years. She was bent over and could not straighten up at all.

- Many spirits are **amplifiers** - they amplify a specific characteristic

Sin, discipline and repentance

- **The 5 Step Process of Man**

(1) Man made in God's image

- **Gen 1:27 (ESV)** - So God created man in his own image, in the image of God he created him; male and female he created them.

(2) Man sinned

- **Gen 3:6-7a (NIV) -** [6] When the woman saw that the fruit of the tree [*of the knowledge of good and evil*] was good for food and pleasing to the eye, and also desirable for gaining wisdom, she took some and ate it. She also gave some to her husband, who was with her, and he ate it. [7] Then the eyes of both of them were opened...

(3) Man lost God's image

- **Gen 5:3 (ESV)** - When Adam had lived 130 years, he fathered a son in *his* own likeness, after his image, and named him Seth.

(4) Jesus made in God's image

- **Rom 8:3 (ESV)** - For what the Law could not do, weak as it was through the flesh, God did: sending His own Son in the likeness of sinful flesh and as an offering for sin, He condemned sin in the flesh

- **Heb 1:3a (ESV)** - He is the radiance of the glory of God and the exact imprint of his nature, and he upholds the universe by the word of his power...

- **We are to be conformed to Jesus's image ... *God's* image**
- **Rom 8:29 (ESV)** - For those whom he foreknew he also predestined to be conformed to the image of his Son, in order that he might be the firstborn among many brothers

- **Question:** How do we conform to the image of his Son?
- **Answer:** Repent of our sin

(5) Man repents to restore God's image

- When we repent of our sin, it removes the sin
  --> this was Jesus's primary message

- Repentance **is the primary message throughout the Bible**

  - **God in OT --> Joel 2:12-13 (ESV)** - [12] "Yet even now," declares the LORD, "return to me with all your heart ["repent"], with fasting, with weeping, and with mourning; [13] and rend your hearts and not your garments." Return to the LORD your God, for he is gracious and merciful, slow to anger, and abounding in steadfast love; and he relents over disaster.

- **John the Baptist --> Mat 3:1-2 (ESV)** - In those days John the Baptist came preaching in the wilderness of Judea, [2] "Repent, for the kingdom of heaven is at hand."
- **Jesus --> Mat 4:17 (ESV)** - From that time Jesus began to preach, saying, "Repent, for the kingdom of heaven is at hand."

- **Sin does two things**

  1. breaks relationship with God

     → to restore: repent of sins as a whole

  2. breaks image of God

     → to restore: repent of sins individually

- **God and Michelangelo - a picture of what this looks like**
  - God conform us back to his image in the same way Michelangelo created beautiful sculptures --> one chip at a time
  - **Luk 6:40 (ESV)** - A disciple is not above his teacher, but everyone when he is fully trained will be like his teacher.

Session 3: A walk through the Bible (part 1) Answer Key

Spiritual laws vs God's covenants

- Many of God's spiritual laws operate *outside* of his covenants with man
- **Example 1 Seventh Day:** God declared the seventh day holy
- **Example 2 Tithe:** God declares the tithe ("a 10th part") is holy
- **God's spiritual laws of sin and discipline are the** same
- **Malachi 3:6 (NIV)** - "I the LORD do not change...
- **James 1:17 (NIV)** - Every good and perfect gift is from above, coming down from the Father of the heavenly lights, who does not change...

A walk through the Bible - sin and discipline

OLD TESTAMENT

- **(1) Miriam and leprosy: Num 12:1-10** (NIV) - [1] Miriam and Aaron began
to talk against Moses because of his Cushite wife, for he had married a Cushite. [2]
"Has the LORD spoken only through Moses?" they asked. "Hasn't he also spoken
through us?" And the LORD heard this. [3] (Now Moses was a very humble man,
more humble than anyone else on the face of the earth.) [4] At once the LORD said
to Moses, Aaron and Miriam, "Come out to the tent of meeting, all three of you."
So the three of them went out. [5] Then the LORD came down in a pillar of cloud; he
stood at the entrance to the tent and summoned Aaron and Miriam. When the
two of them stepped forward, [6] he said, "Listen to my words: "When there is a
prophet among you, I, the LORD, reveal myself to them in visions, I speak to them
in dreams. [7] But this is not true of my servant Moses; he is faithful in all my
house. [8] With him I speak face to face, clearly and not in riddles; he sees the form
of the LORD. Why then were you not afraid to speak against my servant Moses?" [9]
The anger of the LORD burned against them, and he left them. [10] When the cloud
lifted from above the tent, Miriam's skin was leprous—it became as white as
snow...

- **(2) Venomous snakes: Num 21:4-7a (NIV) -** [4] "They traveled from Mount Hor ... but the people grew impatient on the way; [5] they spoke against God... [6] Then the LORD sent venomous snakes among them; they bit the people and many Israelites died. [7] The people came to Moses and said, 'We sinned when we spoke against the LORD ...'"

- **(3) Life of lack: Deu 28:15-20 (NIV) -** [15] However, if you do not obey the LORD your God and do not carefully follow all his commands and decrees I am giving you today, all these curses will come on you and overtake you: [16] You will be cursed in the city and cursed in the country. [17] Your basket and your kneading trough will be cursed. [18] The fruit of your womb will be cursed, and the crops of your land, and the calves of your herds and the lambs of your flocks. [19] You will be cursed when you come in and cursed when you go out. [20] The LORD will send on you curses, confusion and rebuke in everything you put your hand to...

- **(4) Diseases of Egypt: Deu 28:58-61 (NIV) -** [58] "If you do not carefully follow all the words of this law, which are written in this book, and do not revere this glorious and awesome name —the LORD your God— [59] the LORD will send fearful plagues on you and your descendants, harsh and prolonged disasters, and severe and lingering illnesses. [60] He will bring on you all the diseases of Egypt that you dreaded, and they will cling to you. [61] The LORD will also bring on you every kind of sickness and disaster not recorded in this Book of the Law..."

- **(5) Jeroboam's hand shrivels: 1 Kings 13:1-4 (NIV) -** [1] By the word of the LORD a man of God came from Judah to Bethel, as Jeroboam was standing by the altar to make an offering. [2] By the word of the LORD he cried out against the altar: "Altar, altar! This is what the LORD says: 'A son named Josiah will be born to the house of David. On you he will sacrifice the priests of the high places who make offerings here, and human bones will be burned on you.'" [3] That same day the man of God gave a sign: "This is the sign the LORD has declared: The altar will be split apart and the ashes on it will be poured out." [4] When King Jeroboam heard what the man of God cried out against the altar at Bethel, he stretched out his hand from the altar and said, "Seize him!" But the hand he stretched out toward the man shriveled up, so that he could not pull it back.

- **(6) Gehazi and leprosy: 2 Kings 5:14-27 (NIV) -** [14] So [Naaman, the Syrian] went down and dipped himself in the Jordan seven times, as [Elisha] the man of God had told him, and his flesh was restored and became clean like that of a young boy. [15] Then Naaman and all his attendants went back to the man of God . He stood before him and said, "Now I know that there is no God in all the world except in Israel. So please accept a gift from your servant." [16] The prophet answered, "As surely as the LORD lives, whom I serve, I will not accept a thing." And even though Naaman urged him, he refused... [*Naaman leaves and goes a* *short way*]... 21 So Gehazi [Elisha's servant] hurried after Naaman. When Naaman saw him running toward him, he got down from the chariot to meet him. "Is everything all right?" he asked. 22 "Everything is all right," Gehazi answered. "My master sent me to say, 'Two young men from the company of the prophets have just come to me from the hill country of Ephraim. Please give them a talent of silver and two sets of clothing.'" 23 "By all means, take two talents," said Naaman. He urged Gehazi to accept them, and then tied up the two talents of silver in two bags, with two sets of clothing. He gave them to two of his servants, and they carried them ahead of Gehazi. 24 When Gehazi came to the hill, he took the things from the servants and put them away in the house. He sent the men away and they left. 25 When he went in and stood before his master, Elisha asked him, "Where have you been, Gehazi?" "Your servant didn't go anywhere," Gehazi answered. 26 But Elisha said to him, "Was not my spirit with you when the man got down from his chariot to meet you? Is this the time to take money or to accept clothes—or olive groves and vineyards, or flocks and herds, or male and female slaves? 27 Naaman's leprosy will cling to you and to your descendants forever." Then Gehazi went from Elisha's presence and his skin was leprous—it had become as white as snow.

- **(7) Uzziah and leprosy: 2 Chr 26:16-21 (NIV) -** 16 But after Uzziah became powerful, his pride led to his downfall. He was unfaithful to the LORD his God, and entered the temple of the LORD to burn incense on the altar of incense. 17 Azariah the priest with eighty other courageous priests of the LORD followed him in. 18 They confronted King Uzziah and said, "It is not right for you, Uzziah, to burn incense to the LORD. That is for the priests, the descendants of Aaron, who have been consecrated to burn incense. Leave the sanctuary, for you have been unfaithful; and you will not be honored by the LORD God." 19 Uzziah, who had a censer in his hand ready to burn incense, became angry. While he was raging at the priests in their presence before the incense altar in the LORD's temple, leprosy broke out on his forehead. 20 When Azariah the chief priest and all the other priests looked at him, they saw that he had leprosy on his forehead, so they hurried him out. Indeed, he himself was eager to leave, because the LORD had afflicted him. 21 King Uzziah had leprosy until the day he died. He lived in a separate house —leprous, and banned from the temple of the LORD...

- **(8) King David infirmed: Psalms 32:1-4 (NLT) -** 1 Oh, what joy for those whose disobedience is forgiven, whose sin is put out of sight! 2 Yes, what joy for those whose record the LORD has cleared of guilt, whose lives are lived in complete honesty! 3 When I refused to confess my sin, my body wasted away, and I groaned all day long. 4 Day and night your hand of discipline was heavy on me. My strength evaporated like water in the summer heat.

Session 4: A walk through the Bible (part 2) Answer Key

NEW TESTAMENT

- **(9) Woman with spirit of infirmity: Luk 13:10-13 (NIV)** - On a Sabbath Jesus was teaching in one of the synagogues, and a woman was there who had been crippled by a spirit for eighteen years. She was bent over and could not straighten up at all. When Jesus saw her, he called her forward and said to her, "Woman, you are set free from your infirmity." Then he put his hands on her, and immediately she straightened up and praised God.
    - It was due to sin -- how do we know? ...
    - Why did Jesus tell this man, "Sin no more, that nothing worse may happen to you?"

      Luk 13:14-16 (NIV) - [14] Indignant because Jesus had healed on the Sabbath, the synagogue leader said to the people, "There are six days for work. So come and be healed on those days, not on the Sabbath." [15] The Lord answered him, "You hypocrites! Doesn't each of you on the Sabbath untie your ox or donkey from the stall and lead it out to give it water? [16] Then should not this woman, a daughter of Abraham, whom Satan has kept bound for eighteen long years, be set free on the Sabbath day from what bound her?"

- **(10) Lame man at the pool: Joh 5:2-9,14 (ESV)** - [2] "Now there is in Jerusalem by the Sheep Gate a pool, in Aramaic called Bethesda, which has five roofed colonnades. [3] In these lay a multitude of invalids—blind, lame, and paralyzed. [5] One man was there who had been an invalid for thirty-eight years. [6] When Jesus saw him lying there and knew that he had already been there a long time... [8] Jesus said to him, 'Get up, take up your bed, and walk.' [9] And at once the man was healed, and he took up his bed and walked.... [14] Afterward Jesus found him in the temple and said to him, 'See, you are well! Sin no more, that nothing worse may happen to you.'"

    - **Question:** Why did Jesus tell this man, "Sin no more, that nothing worse may happen to you?

    - **Answer:** because sin can be a root of infirmity

- **(11) Herod Agrippa: Act 12:21-23 (NIV)** - [21] On the appointed day Herod, wearing his royal robes, sat on his throne and delivered a public address to the people. [22] They shouted, "This is the voice of a god, not of a man." [23] Immediately, because Herod did not give praise to God, an angel of the Lord struck him down, and he was eaten by worms and died.

- **(12) Ananias lies to God: Acts 5:1-5 (NIV)** - [1] Now a man named Ananias, together with his wife Sapphira, also sold a piece of property. [2] With his wife's full knowledge he kept back part of the money for himself, but brought the rest and put it at the apostles' feet. [3] Then Peter said, "Ananias, how is it that Satan has so filled your heart that you have lied to the Holy Spirit and have kept for yourself some of the money you received for the land? [4] Didn't it belong to you before it was sold? And after it was sold, wasn't the money at your disposal? What made you think of doing such a thing? You have not lied just to human beings but to God." [5] When Ananias heard this, he fell down and died. And great fear seized all who heard what had happened.

- **(13) Man with father's wife: 1 Corinthians 5:1-5 (NIV)** - [1] It is actually reported that there is sexual immorality among you, and of a kind that even pagans do not tolerate: A man is sleeping with his father's wife. [2] And you are proud! Shouldn't you rather have gone into mourning and have put out of your fellowship the man who has been doing this? [3] For my part, even though I am not physically present, I am with you in spirit. As one who is present with you in this way, I have already passed judgment in the name of our Lord Jesus on the one who has been doing this. [4] So when you are assembled and I am with you in spirit, and the power of our Lord Jesus is present, [5] hand this man over to Satan for the destruction of the flesh, so that his spirit may be saved on the day of the Lord.

- **(14) Lord's supper: 1 Cor 11:29-30 (NIV)** - [29] "For those who eat and drink without discerning the body of Christ eat and drink judgment on themselves. [30] That is why many among you are weak and sick, and a number of you have fallen asleep."
    - **1 Cor 11:32 (NIV)** - "... when we are judged in this way by the Lord, we are being **disciplined** so that we will not be finally condemned with the world."

- **(15) Call for the elders: Jam 5:14-16 (ESV)** - [14] "Is anyone among you sick? Let him call for the elders of the church, and let them pray over him, anointing him with oil in the name of the Lord. [15] And the prayer of faith will save the one who is sick, and the Lord will raise him up. And if he has committed sins, he will be forgiven. [16] Therefore, confess your sins to one another... that you may be healed. The prayer of a righteous person has great power as it is working."

Sickness vs Sin

- **Not all sickness is due to sin** --> some can come from natural causes

- **What about the blind man?**
    - **Joh 9:1-3 (NIV) -** [1] As he went along, he saw a man blind from birth. [2] His disciples asked him, "Rabbi, who sinned, this man or his parents, that he was born blind?" [3] "Neither this man nor his parents sinned," said Jesus, "but this happened so that the works of God might be displayed in him.

- **What if you've lived a sinful life and have lots of issues?**
    - **Isaiah 46:12-13 (NLT)** - "Listen to me, you stubborn people who are so far from doing right. For I am ready to set things right, not in the distant future, but right now! I am ready to save Jerusalem and show my glory to Israel.

Healing vs God's will

- **1 Joh 5:14-15 (NIV) -** [14] This is the confidence we have in approaching God: that if we ask anything according to his will, he hears us. [15] And if we know that he hears us—whatever we ask—we know that we have what we asked of him.

- **2 Pet 3:9 (NIV) -** The Lord is not slow in keeping his promise, as some understand slowness. Instead he is patient with you, not wanting anyone to perish, but everyone to come to repentance.

Conclusion

- God's word is clear -- our sins produce earthly consequences
- **Joh 10:10 (ESV) -** "The thief comes only to steal and kill and destroy. I came that they may have life and have it abundantly."

Question: How do you get that abundant life?

Answer: By repenting of your sin

- **Mal 3:6-12 (NIV) -** [6] "I the LORD do not change. So you, the descendants of Jacob, are not destroyed. [7] Ever since the time of your ancestors you have turned away from my decrees and have not kept them. Return to me, and I will return to you," says the LORD Almighty. "But you ask, 'How are we to return?' [8] "Will a mere mortal rob God? Yet you rob me. "But you ask, 'How are we robbing you?' "In tithes and offerings. [9] You are under a curse —your whole nation—because you are robbing me. [10] Bring the whole tithe into the storehouse, that there may be food in my house. Test me in this," says the LORD Almighty, "and see if I will not throw open the floodgates of heaven and pour out so much blessing that there will not be room enough to store it. [11] I will prevent pests from devouring your crops, and the vines in your fields will not drop their fruit before it is ripe, " says the LORD Almighty. [12] "Then all the nations will call you blessed, for yours will be a delightful land," says the LORD Almighty.

When you repent from sin, God promises the discipline will be stopped and abundance will be restored

Session 5: Parable of the Unmerciful Servant – Answer Key

Isn't suffering good for us?

- **2 types of suffering**
  - Disobedience --> discipline -- YES stop
  - Obedience --> persecution -- NO stop

Parable of the Unmerciful Servant

Mat 18:21-35 (NIV) -

21 Then Peter came to Jesus and asked, "Lord, how many times shall I
forgive my brother or sister who sins against me? Up to seven times?" 22
Jesus answered, "I tell you, not seven times, but seventy-seven times.

23 "Therefore, the kingdom of heaven is like a king who wanted to settle
accounts with his servants. 24 As he began the settlement, a man who
owed him ten thousand bags of gold was brought to him. 25 Since he was
not able to pay, the master ordered that he and his wife and his children
and all that he had be sold to repay the debt. 26 "At this the servant fell on
his knees before him. 'Be patient with me,' he begged, 'and I will pay back
everything.' 27 The servant's master took pity on him, canceled the debt
and let him go.

28 "But when that servant went out, he found one of his fellow servants
who owed him a hundred silver coins. He grabbed him and began to
choke him. 'Pay back what you owe me!' he demanded. 29 "His fellow
servant fell to his knees and begged him, 'Be patient with me, and I will
pay it back.' 30 "But he refused. Instead, he went off and had the man
thrown into prison until he could pay the debt.

31 When the other servants saw what had happened, they were outraged
and went and told their master everything that had happened. 32 "Then
the master called the servant in. 'You wicked servant,' he said, 'I canceled
all that debt of yours because you begged me to. 33 Shouldn't you have had
mercy on your fellow servant just as I had on you?' 34 In anger his master

handed him over to the jailers to be **tortured**, until he should pay back all he owed.

35 "This is how my heavenly Father **will** treat each of you unless you forgive your brother or sister from your heart."

- **Greek for "torturer"** (also translated as "jailer") -- means "one who elicits the truth by the use of the rack"

  - Root "basanizo" meaning: **to torture** -- pain, toil, torment

(1) Mat 8:5-6 - When he had entered Capernaum, a centurion came forward to him, appealing to him, "Lord, my servant is lying paralyzed at home, suffering terribly." -- **physical suffering**

(2) 2 Pet 2:7-8 - and if he rescued righteous Lot, greatly distressed by the sensual conduct of the wicked (for as that righteous man lived among them day after day, he was tormenting his righteous soul over their lawless deeds that he saw and heard) -- **mental suffering**

(3) Rev 12:2 - She was pregnant and was crying out in birth pains and the agony of giving birth -- **physical pain**

Session 6: Legal Rights – Answer Key

A practical look at spiritual warfare

- **Eph 6:12 (ESV)** - For we do not wrestle against flesh and blood, but against the rulers, against the authorities, against the cosmic powers over this present darkness, against the spiritual forces of evil in the heavenly places.
    - **Eph 6:12 (TLB)** - For we are not fighting against people made of flesh and blood, but against persons without bodies...

Legal structure is part of God's design

- **Eph 1:20-21 (ESV)** - " [20] ...when [God] raised him [Jesus] from the dead and seated him at his right hand in the heavenly places, [21] far above all rule and authority and power and dominion, and above every name that is named..."
- **Mat 28:18 (ESV)** - "And Jesus came and said to them, "All authority in heaven and on earth has been given to me.'"
- **Job 1:6 (ESV)** - "Now there was a day when the sons of God came to present themselves before the LORD, and Satan also came among them"
- **Heb 12:22-24 (ESV)** - "[22] But you have come to Mount Zion and to the city of the living God, the heavenly Jerusalem, and to innumerable angels in festal gathering, [23] and to the assembly of the firstborn who are enrolled in heaven, and to God, the judge of all, and to the spirits of the righteous made perfect, [24] and to Jesus, the mediator of a new covenant, and to the sprinkled blood that speaks a better word than the blood of Abel"

Unrepented Sins and Legal Rights

4 Steps of a Deliverance

1. Identify
2. Interrogate
3. Repent
4. Command Out

Evidence of Legal Rights in scripture

- **Col 2:13c-15 (ESV) -** " 13 ... [Jesus] having forgiven us all our trespasses, 14 by canceling the record of debt that stood against us with its legal demands. This he set aside, nailing it to the cross. 15 He disarmed the rulers and authorities and put them to open shame, by triumphing over them in him."

- **Job: Job 1:6-12 -** " 6 Now there was a day when the sons of God came to present themselves before the LORD, and Satan also came among them. 7 The LORD said to Satan, "From where have you come?" Satan answered the LORD and said, "From going to and fro on the earth, and from walking up and down on it." 8 And the LORD said to Satan, "Have you considered my servant Job, that there is none like him on the earth, a blameless and upright man, who fears God and turns away from evil?" 9 Then Satan answered the LORD and said, "Does Job fear God for no reason? 10 Have you not put **a hedge around him** and his house and all that he has, on every side? You have blessed the work of his hands, and his possessions have increased in the land. 11 But stretch out your hand and touch all that he has, and he will curse you to your face." 12 And the LORD said to Satan, "Behold, all that he has is in your hand. Only against him do not stretch out your hand." So Satan went out from the presence of the LORD."

  - **Job 1:4-5 -** " 4 His sons used to go and hold a feast in the house of each one on his day, and they would send and invite their three sisters to eat and drink with them. 5 And when the days of the feast had run their course, Job would send and consecrate them, and he would rise early in the morning and offer burnt offerings according to the number of them all. For Job said, "It may be that my children have sinned, and cursed God in their hearts." Thus Job did continually."

What spiritual attacks look like

[Diagram]

Act 3:19 (NIV) - "Repent, then, and turn to God, so that your sins may be wiped out, that times of refreshing may come from the Lord"

- repenting of sins brings refreshing times now

www.ingramcontent.com/pod-product-compliance
Lightning Source LLC
Chambersburg PA
CBHW081251130726
47998CB00010B/2754

* 9 7 9 8 9 8 9 0 5 9 1 2 6 *